CCNA Routing and Switching Practice and Study Guide:
Exercises, Activities, and Scenarios to Prepare for the ICND2 (200-101) Certification Exam

Allan Johnson

Cisco Press

800 East 96th Street

Indianapolis, Indiana 46240 USA

CCNA Routing and Switching Practice and Study Guide:

Exercises, Activities, and Scenarios to Prepare for the ICND2 (200-101) Certification Exam

Student Edition

Allan Johnson

Copyright© 2014 Cisco Systems, Inc.

Cisco Press logo is a trademark of Cisco Systems, Inc.

Published by:
Cisco Press
800 East 96th Street
Indianapolis, IN 46240 USA

Printed in the United States of America

First Printing April 2014

ISBN-13: 978-1-58713-344-2

ISBN-10: 1-58713-344-X

Library of Congress Control Number: 2014933142

Warning and Disclaimer

This book is designed to provide information about networking. Every effort has been made to make this book as complete and as accurate as possible, but no warranty or fitness is implied.

The information is provided on an "as is" basis. The authors, Cisco Press, and Cisco Systems, Inc. shall have neither liability nor responsibility to any person or entity with respect to any loss or damages arising from the information contained in this book or from the use of the discs or programs that may accompany it.

The opinions expressed in this book belong to the author and are not necessarily those of Cisco Systems, Inc.

Publisher
Paul Boger

Associate Publisher
Dave Dusthimer

Business Operation Manager, Cisco Press
Jan Cornelssen

Executive Editor
Mary Beth Ray

Managing Editor
Sandra Schroeder

Senior Development Editor
Christopher Cleveland

Project Editor
Mandie Frank

Copy Editor
Keith Cline

Technical Editor
Steve Stiles

Editorial Assistant
Vanessa Evans

Designer
Mark Shirar

Composition
Tricia Bronkella

Proofreader
Sarah Kearns

Trademark Acknowledgments

All terms mentioned in this book that are known to be trademarks or service marks have been appropriately capitalized. Cisco Press or Cisco Systems, Inc. cannot attest to the accuracy of this information. Use of a term in this book should not be regarded as affecting the validity of any trademark or service mark.

Special Sales

For information about buying this title in bulk quantities, or for special sales opportunities (which may include electronic versions; custom cover designs; and content particular to your business, training goals, marketing focus, or branding interests), please contact our corporate sales department at corpsales@pearsoned.com or (800) 382-3419.

For government sales inquiries, please contact governmentsales@pearsoned.com.

For questions about sales outside the U.S., please contact international@pearsoned.com.

Feedback Information

At Cisco Press, our goal is to create in-depth technical books of the highest quality and value. Each book is crafted with care and precision, undergoing rigorous development that involves the unique expertise of members from the professional technical community.

Readers' feedback is a natural continuation of this process. If you have any comments regarding how we could improve the quality of this book, or otherwise alter it to better suit your needs, you can contact us through email at feedback@ciscopress.com. Please make sure to include the book title and ISBN in your message.

We greatly appreciate your assistance.

Americas Headquarters	Asia Pacific Headquarters	Europe Headquarters
Cisco Systems, Inc.	Cisco Systems, Inc.	Cisco Systems International BV
170 West Tasman Drive	168 Robinson Road	Haarlerbergpark
San Jose, CA 95134-1706	#28-01 Capital Tower	Haarlerbergweg 13-19
USA	Singapore 068912	1101 CH Amsterdam
www.cisco.com	www.cisco.com	The Netherlands
Tel: 408 526-4000	Tel: +65 6317 7777	www-europe.cisco.com
800 553-NETS (6387)	Fax: +65 6317 7799	Tel: +31 0 800 020 0791
Fax: 408 527-0883		Fax: +31 0 20 357 1100

Cisco has more than 200 offices worldwide. Addresses, phone numbers, and fax numbers are listed on the Cisco Website at www.cisco.com/go/offices.

©2008 Cisco Systems, Inc. All rights reserved. CCVP, the Cisco logo, and the Cisco Square Bridge logo are trademarks of Cisco Systems, Inc.; Changing the Way We Work, Live, Play, and Learn is a service mark of Cisco Systems, Inc.; and Access Registrar, Aironet, BPX, Catalyst, CCDA, CCDP, CCIE, CCIP, CCNA, CCNP, CCSP, Cisco, the Cisco Certified Internetwork Expert logo, Cisco IOS, Cisco Press, Cisco Systems, Cisco Systems Capital, the Cisco Systems logo, Cisco Unity, Enterprise/Solver, EtherChannel, EtherFast, EtherSwitch, Fast Step, Follow Me Browsing, FormShare, GigaDrive, GigaStack, HomeLink, Internet Quotient, IOS, IP/TV, iQ Expertise, the iQ logo, iQ Net Readiness Scorecard, iQuick Study, LightStream, Linksys, MeetingPlace, MGX, Networking Academy, Network Registrar, Packet, PIX, ProConnect, RateMUX, ScriptShare, SlideCast, SMARTnet, StackWise, The Fastest Way to Increase Your Internet Quotient, and TransPath are registered trademarks of Cisco Systems, Inc. and/or its affiliates in the United States and certain other countries.

All other trademarks mentioned in this document or Website are the property of their respective owners. The use of the word partner does not imply a partnership relationship between Cisco and any other company. (0609R)

About the Author

Allan Johnson entered the academic world in 1999 after 10 years as a business owner/operator to dedicate his efforts to his passion for teaching. He holds both an MBA and an M.Ed in Occupational Training and Development. He is an information technology instructor at Del Mar College in Corpus Christi, Texas. In 2003, Allan began to commit much of his time and energy to the CCNA Instructional Support Team, providing services to Networking Academy instructors worldwide and creating training materials. He now works full time for Cisco Networking Academy as a Learning Systems Developer.

About the Technical Reviewer

Steve Stiles is a Cisco Network Academy Instructor for Rhodes State College and a Cisco Certified Instructor Trainer, having earned CCNA Security and CCNP level certifications. He was the recipient of the 2012 Outstanding Teacher of the Year by the Ohio Association of Two-Year Colleges and co-recipient for the Outstanding Faculty of the Year at Rhodes State College.

Dedication

For my wife, Becky. Without the sacrifices you made during the project, this work would not have come to fruition. Thank you providing me the comfort and resting place only you can give.

—Allan Johnson

Acknowledgments

When I began to think of whom I would like to have as a technical editor for this work, Steve Stiles immediately came to mind. With his instructor and industry background, and his excellent work building activities for the new Cisco Networking Academy curriculum, he was an obvious choice. Thankfully, when Mary Beth Ray contacted him, he was willing and able to do the arduous review work necessary to make sure that you get a book that is both technically accurate and unambiguous.

The Cisco Network Academy authors for the online curriculum and series of Companion Guides take the reader deeper, past the CCENT exam topics, with the ultimate goal of not only preparing the student for CCENT certification, but for more advanced college-level technology courses and degrees, as well. Thank you especially to Amy Gerrie and her team of authors— Rick Graziani, Wayne Lewis, and Bob Vachon—for their excellent treatment of the material; it is reflected throughout this book.

Mary Beth Rey, Executive Editor, you amaze me with your ability to juggle multiple projects at once, steering each from beginning to end. I can always count on you to make the tough decisions.

This is my seventh project with Christopher Cleveland as development editor. His dedication to perfection pays dividends in countless, unseen ways. Thank you again, Chris, for providing me with much-needed guidance and support. This book could not be a reality without your persistence.

Contents at a Glance

Contents

Icons Used in This Book

 Router

 Bridge

 Hub

 DSU/CSU

 Catalyst Switch

 Multilayer Switch

 ATM Switch

 ISDN/Frame Relay Switch

 Communication Server

 Gateway

Access Server

Command Syntax Conventions

The conventions used to present command syntax in this book are the same conventions used in the IOS Command Reference. The Command Reference describes these conventions as follows:

- **Boldface** indicates commands and keywords that are entered literally as shown. In actual configuration examples and output (not general command syntax), boldface indicates commands that are manually input by the user (such as a **show** command).

- *Italics* indicate arguments for which you supply actual values.

- Vertical bars (|) separate alternative, mutually exclusive elements.

- Square brackets [ ] indicate optional elements.

- Braces { } indicate a required choice.

- Braces within brackets [{ }] indicate a required choice within an optional element.

Introduction

The purpose of this book is to provide you with an extra resource for studying the exam topics of the Interconnecting Cisco Networking Devices Part 2 (ICND2) exam that leads to Cisco Certified Networking Associate (CCNA) certification. This book maps to the third and fourth Cisco Networking Academy courses in the CCNA Routing and Switching curricula: *Scaling Networks* (SN) and *Connecting Networks* (CN). Ideally, the reader will have completed the first two courses: *Introduction to Networks* (ITN) and *Routing and Switching Essentials* (RSE). SN continues where RSE left off, taking the student deeper into the architecture, components, and operations of routers and switches in a large and complex network. Successfully completing this course means that you should be able to configure and troubleshoot routers and switches and resolve common issues with OSPF, EIGRP, STP, and VTP in both IPv4 and IPv6 networks. CN pulls everything from the first three courses together as the student learns the WAN technologies and network services required by converged applications in a complex network. Successfully completing this course means that you should be able to configure and troubleshoot network devices and resolve common WAN issues and implement IPsec and virtual private network (VPN) operations in a complex network. To learn more about CCNA Routing and Switching courses and to find an Academy near you, visit http://www.netacad.com.

However, if you are not an Academy student but would like to benefit from the extensive authoring done for these courses, you can buy any or all of CCNA Routing and Switching Companion Guides (CG) and Lab Manuals (LM) of the Academy's popular online curriculum. Although you will not have access to the Packet Tracer network simulator software, you will have access to the tireless work of an outstanding team of Cisco Academy instructors dedicated to providing students with comprehensive and engaging CCNA Routing and Switching preparation course material. The titles and ISBNs for the first two courses of the CCNA Routing and Switching CGs and LMs are as follows:

- *Scaling Networks Companion Guide* (ISBN: 9781587133282)
- *Scaling Networks Lab Manual* (ISBN: 9781587133251)
- *Connecting Networks Companion Guide* (ISBN: 9781587133329)
- *Connecting Networks Lab Manual* (ISBN: 9781587133312)

Goals and Methods

The most important goal of this book is to help you pass the 200-101 Interconnecting Cisco Networking Devices Part 2 (ICND2) exam, which is associated with the Cisco Certified Network Associate (CCNA) certification. Passing the CCNA exam means that you have the knowledge and skills required to successfully install, operate, and troubleshoot a small branch office network. You can view the detailed exam topics any time at http://learningnetwork.cisco.com. They are divided into five broad categories:

- LAN Switching Technologies
- IP Routing Technologies
- IP Services
- Troubleshooting
- WAN Technologies

This book offers exercises that help you learn the concepts, configurations, and troubleshooting skills crucial to your success as a CCNA exam candidate. Each chapter differs slightly and includes some or all of the following types of practice:

- Vocabulary-matching exercises
- Concept question exercises
- Skill-building activities and scenarios
- Configuration scenarios
- Troubleshooting scenarios

Audience for This Book

This book's main audience is anyone taking the CCNA Routing and Switching courses of the Cisco Networking Academy curriculum. Many Academies use this Practice Study Guide as a required tool in the course, whereas other Academies recommend the Practice Study Guide as an additional resource to prepare for class exams and the CCNA certification.

The secondary audiences for this book include people taking CCNA-related classes from professional training organizations. This book can also be used for college- and university-level networking courses, and by anyone wanting to gain a detailed understanding of INCD2 routing and switching concepts.

How This Book Is Organized

Because the content of the *Scaling Networks Companion Guide*, the *Connecting Networks Companion Guide*, and the online curriculum is sequential, you should work through this Practice and Study Guide in order beginning with Chapter 1.

The book covers the major topic headings in the same sequence as the online curriculum. This book has 18 chapters, their names the same as the online course chapters. However, the numbering is sequential in this book, progressing from Chapter 1 to Chapter 18. The online curriculum starts over at Chapter 1 in the *Connecting Networks* course.

Most of the configuration chapters use a single topology where appropriate. This allows for better continuity and easier understanding of routing and switching commands, operations, and outputs. However, the topology differs from the one used in the online curriculum and the Companion Guide. A different topology affords you the opportunity to practice your knowledge and skills without just simply recording the information you find in the text.

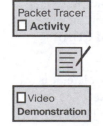

Packet Tracer
☐ Activity

☐ Video
Demonstration

Note: Throughout the book, you will find references to Packet Tracer and Lab activities. These references are provided so that you can, at that point, complete those activities. The Packet Tracer activities are accessible only if you have access to the online curriculum. However, the Labs are available in the Lab Manuals previously cited.

Part I: Scaling Networks

- **Chapter 1, "Introduction to Scaling Networks":** This chapter provides vocabulary and concept exercises to reinforce your understanding of hierarchical network design and selecting hardware. You will also practice basic router and switch configuration and verification.

- **Chapter 2, "LAN Redundancy":** The exercises in this chapter cover the concepts, operations, configuration, and verification of all the current varieties of STP.

- **Chapter 3, "Link Aggregation":** This chapter's exercises are devoted to the concepts, configuration, verification, and troubleshooting of EtherChannel.

- **Chapter 4, "Wireless LANs":** This chapter is all about wireless connectivity technologies. You will complete exercises that focus on various types of wireless and the standards for 802.11. In addition, you will complete activities focused on WLAN components, topologies, and security.

- **Chapter 5, "Adjust and Troubleshoot Single-Area OSPF":** This chapter focuses on advanced OSPF concepts, configuration, verification, and troubleshooting.

- **Chapter 6, "Multiarea OSPF":** The CCNA exam now includes multiarea OSPF. So, this chapter includes exercises covering multiarea OSPF concepts and configuration, verification, and troubleshooting.

- **Chapter 7, "EIGRP":** The exercises in this chapter are devoted to the basic concepts and configuration of Cisco's routing protocol, EIGRP for IPv4 and IPv6.

- **Chapter 8, "EIGRP Advanced Configurations and Troubleshooting":** This chapter focuses on advanced EIGRP concepts, configuration, verification, and troubleshooting.

- **Chapter 9, "IOS Images and Licensing":** This chapter is devoted to the crucial knowledge and skills you need to manage IOS images. Exercises focus on basic IOS image concepts and management tasks.

Part II: Connecting Networks

- **Chapter 10, "Hierarchical Network Design":** Part II, much like Part I, starts off network design. Exercises focus on the various types of network design models and architectures.

- **Chapter 11, "Connecting to the WAN":** This chapter is a survey of all the various WAN access options and technologies that are available for connecting today's networks. The exercises focus on differentiating between all these WAN options.

- **Chapter 12, "Point-to-Point Connections":** One of the older, and still viable, WAN options is PPP. Exercises in this chapter focus on the serial interface and then the concepts, configuration, verification, and troubleshooting of PPP with PAP and CHAP authentication.

- **Chapter 13, "Frame Relay":** Although some may consider Frame Relay obsolete, it is still a viable option in depending on your location. This chapter includes exercises covering the concepts, configuration, verification, and troubleshooting of Frame Relay.

- **Chapter 14, "Network Address Translation for IPv4"**: NAT was created to provide a temporary solution to the limited address space in IPv4. Just about every router connected to the network uses NAT or forwards traffic to a NAT-enabled device for address translation. This chapter focuses on exercises to reinforce your understanding of NAT operation and characteristics. Practice activities include configuring, verifying, and troubleshooting static NAT, dynamic NAT, and PAT.

- **Chapter 15, "Broadband Solutions"**: Working from home or away from a central office has largely been made possible by the advent of broadband technologies and VPNs. This exercises in this chapter help you distinguish between the various broadband offerings on the market.

- **Chapter 16, "Securing Site-to-Site Connectivity"**: VPNs allow teleworkers and branch sites connect to the corporate network regardless of the underlying WAN access option. The exercises in this chapter are devoted to the concepts of the various VPN solutions, including IPsec and GRE configuration.

- **Chapter 17, "Monitoring the Network"**: As a network administrator, you are more likely to be managing a network using a variety of tools rather than designing and building them. The exercises in this chapter cover three popular network monitoring tools: syslog, SNMP, and NetFlow.

- Chapter 18, **"Troubleshooting the Network"**: Throughout your CCNA studies, you have practice troubleshooting skills in relation to specific technologies. This chapter reviews troubleshooting methodologies and the tools and commands you use to troubleshoot a network. Troubleshooting is a key skill to fine-tune now that you are close to taking your CCNA exam.

About the Cisco Press Website for This Book

Cisco Press provides additional content that can be accessed by registering your individual book at the ciscopress.com website. Becoming a member and registering is free, and you then gain access to exclusive deals on other resources from Cisco Press.

To register this book, go to http://www.ciscopress.com/bookstore/register.asp and enter the book's ISBN located on the back cover of this book. You'll then be prompted to log in or join ciscopress.com to continue registration.

After you register the book, a link to the supplemental content will be listed on your My Registered Books page.

CHAPTER 1

Introduction to Scaling Networks

As a business grows, so does its networking requirements. To keep pace with a business's expansion and new emerging technologies, a network must be designed to scale. A network that scales well is not only one that can handle growing traffic demands, but also one designed with the inevitable need to expand. This short chapter sets the stage for the rest of the course. This chapter covers the hierarchical network design model, the Cisco Enterprise Architecture modules, and appropriate device selections that you can use to systematically design a highly functional network.

Implementing a Network Design

An enterprise network must be designed to support the exchange of various types of network traffic, including data files, email, IP telephony, and video applications for multiple business units.

Hierarchical Network Design

Users expect enterprise networks to be up _____ percent of the time. To provide this kind of reliability, enterprise class equipment uses _____ power supplies and has failover capabilities.

Describe what failover capability means for enterprise class equipment.

Why should a network be organized so that traffic stays local and is not propagated unnecessarily on to other portions of the network?

Designing a network using the three-layer hierarchical design model helps optimize the network. In Figure 1-1, label the three layers of the hierarchical design model.

Figure 1-1   Hierarchical Design Model

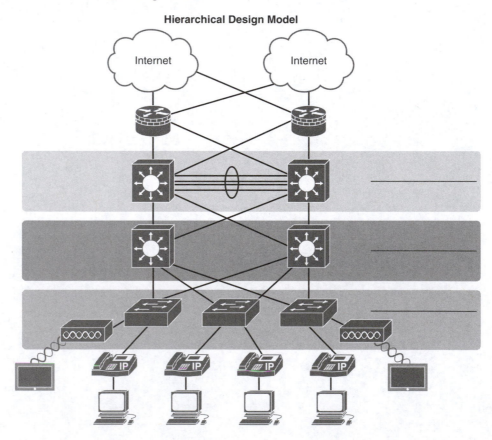

Briefly describe each layer of the hierarchical design model.

The Cisco Enterprise Architecture divides the network into functional components while still maintaining the core, distribution, and access layers. The primary Cisco Enterprise Architecture modules include Enterprise Campus, Enterprise Edge, Service Provider Edge, and Remote.

A well-designed network not only controls traffic but also limits the size of failure domains. Briefly describe a failure domain.

Use the list of modules to label the parts of the Cisco Enterprise Architecture in Figure 1-2.

Modules

1 Campus Core

2 Remote Access & VPN

3 Building Distribution

4 Internet Connectivity

5 Building Access

6 Server Farm & Data Center

7 WAN Site-to-Site VPN

8 E-Commerce

Figure 1-2   Cisco Enterprise Architecture

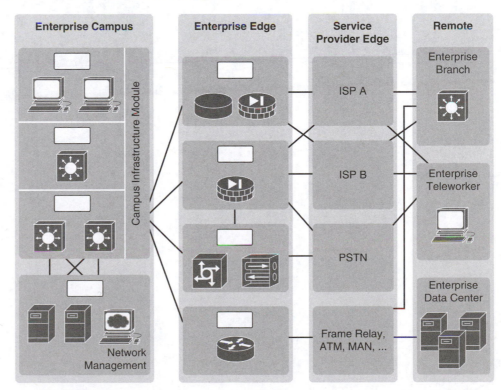

Identify Scalability Terminology

Match the definition on the left with the term on the right. This is a one-to-one matching exercise.

Definition

_____ Isolates routing updates and minimizes the size of routing tables

_____ Cisco proprietary distance vector routing protocol

_____ Allows for redundant paths by eliminating switching loops

_____ Technique for aggregating multiple links between equipment to increase bandwidth

_____ Minimizes the possibility of a single point of failure

_____ Supports new features and devices without requiring major equipment upgrades

_____ Link-state routing protocol with a two-layer hierarchical design

_____ Increases flexibility, reduces costs, and provides mobility to users

Terms

a. Modular equipment

b. OSPF

c. EIGRP

d. Wireless LANs

e. Redundancy

f. Spanning Tree Protocol

g. Scalable Routing Protocol

h. EtherChannel

Selecting Network Devices

When designing a network, it is important to select the proper hardware to meet current network requirements and to allow for network growth. Within an enterprise network, both switches and routers play a critical role in network communication.

Selecting Switch Hardware

Match the business consideration on the left with the switch feature on the right. This is a one-to-one matching exercise.

Business Consideration

_____ Should provide continuous access to the network

_____ Daisy-chain switches with high-bandwidth throughput

_____ Refers to a switch's ability to support the appropriate number of devices on the network

_____ Ability to adjust to growth of network users

_____ How fast the interfaces will process network data

_____ Important consideration in a network where there may be congested ports to servers or other areas of the network

_____ Provides electrical current to other device and support redundant power supplies

_____ Switches with preset features or options

_____ Depends on the number and speed of the interfaces, supported features, and expansion capability

_____ Switches with insertable switching line/port cards

Switch Feature

a. Reliability

b. Modular

c. Power

d. Stackable

e. Frame buffers

f. Cost

g. Fixed configuration

h. Scalability

i. Port speed

j. Port density

Packet Tracer
☐ Activity

Packet Tracer - Comparing 2960 and 3560 Switches (SN 1.2.1.7/SwN 1.1.2.5)

Selecting Router Hardware

In Table 1-1, select the router category that applies to each description.

Table 1-1   **Identify Router Category Features**

Router Description	Branch Routers	Network Edge Routers	Service Provider Routers
Fast performance with high security for data centers, campus, and branch networks			
Simple network configuration and management for LANs and WANs			
Optimizes services on a single platform			
End-to-end delivery of subscriber services			
Deliver next-generation Internet experiences across all devices and locations			
High capacity and scalability with hierarchical quality of service			
Maximizes local services and ensures 24/7/365 uptime			
Unites campus, data center, and branch networks			

Managing Devices

A basic router or switch configuration includes the hostname for identification, passwords for security, and assignment of IP addresses to interfaces for connectivity. A router configuration also includes basic routing.

In addition to configuration commands, router and switch verification commands are used to verify the operational status of the router or switch and related network functionality. Use the address scheme in Table 1-2 in the following exercises that review the most common router and switch configuration and verification commands.

Table 1-2   **Router and Switch Addressing Table**

Device	Interface	IPv4 Address	Subnet Mask	Default Gateway
R1	G0/0	172.16.1.1	255.255.255.0	N/A
	S0/0/0	172.16.3.1	255.255.255.252	N/A
	S0/0/1	192.168.10.5	255.255.255.252	N/A
S1	VLAN 1	192.168.1.5	255.255.255.0	192.168.1.1

Basic Router Configuration Review

Using Table 1-2 and the following requirements, record the commands, including the router prompt, to implement a basic router configuration:

- Hostname is R1.
- Console and Telnet line's password is cisco.
- Privileged EXEC password is class.
- Banner message-of-the-day.
- Interface addressing.
- OSPF routing, including an appropriate router ID.
- Save the configuration.

Router(config)# _____

Basic Router Verification Review

In Table 1-3, record the verification command that will generate the described output.

Table 1-3   Router Verification Commands

Command	Command Output
	Displays the routing table for known networks, including administrative distance, metric, and outbound interface
	Displays information about routing protocols, including process ID, router ID, and neighbors
	Displays information about directly connected Cisco devices
	Displays all interfaces in an abbreviated format, including IP address and status
	Displays information about neighbors, including router ID, state, IP address, and local interface that learned of neighbor
	Displays one or all interfaces, including status, bandwidth, and duplex type

Basic Switch Configuration Review

Using Table 1-2 and the following requirements, record the commands, including the switch prompt, to implement a basic switch configuration:

- Hostname is S1.

- Console and Telnet line's password is cisco.

- Privileged EXEC password is class.

- Banner message-of-the-day.

- VLAN 1 interface addressing.

- Save the configuration.

Switch(config)# _____

_____

_____

_____

_____

_____

_____

_____

_____

_____

_____

_____

_____

_____

_____

_____

Basic Switch Verification Review

In Table 1-4, record the verification command that will generate the described output.

Table 1-4   **Router Verification Commands**

Command	Command Output
	Displays information about directly connected Cisco devices
	Displays all secure MAC addresses
	Displays a table of learned MAC addresses, including the port number and VLAN assigned to the port
	Displays one or all interfaces, including status, bandwidth, and duplex type
	Displays information about maximum MAC addresses allowed, current counts, security violation count, and action to be taken

Packet Tracer - Skills Integration Challenge (SN 1.3.1.2)

CHAPTER 2

LAN Redundancy

Computer networks are inextricably linked to productivity in today's small and medium-sized business-es. Consequently, IT administrators have to implement redundancy in their hierarchical networks. When a switch connection is lost, another link needs to quickly take its place without introducing any traffic loops. This chapter investigates how Spanning Tree Protocol (STP) logically blocks physical loops in the network and how STP has evolved into a robust protocol that rapidly calculates which ports should be blocked in a VLAN-based network. In addition, the chapter briefly explores how Layer 3 redundancy is implemented through First Hop Redundancy Protocols (FHRPs).

Spanning-Tree Concepts

Redundancy increases the availability of a network topology by protecting the network from a single point of failure, such as a failed network cable or switch. STP was developed to address the issue of loops in a redundant Layer 2 design.

Draw a Redundant Topology

In Figure 2-1, draw redundant links between the access, distribution, and core switches. Each access switch should have two links to the distribution layer with each link connecting to a different distribution layer switch. Each distribution layer switch should have two links to the core layer with each link connecting to a different core layer switch.

Figure 2-1   Redundant Topology

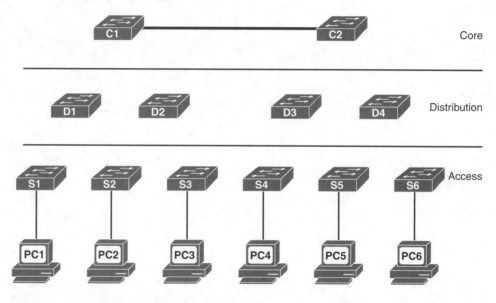

Purpose of Spanning Tree

STP prevents specific types of issues in a redundant topology like the one in Figure 2-1. Specifically, three potential issues would occur if STP was not implemented. Describe each of the following issues:

- MAC database instability:

- Broadcast storms:

- Multiple frame transmission:

You should be prepared to use a topology like Figure 2-1 to explain exactly how these three issues would occur if STP was not implemented.

Packet Tracer ☐ **Activity**

Packet Tracer - Examining a Redundant Design (SN 2.1.1.5/SwN 4.1.1.5)

Spanning-Tree Operation

Because _____ (RSTP), which is documented in IEEE _____ -2004, supersedes the original STP documented in IEEE _____ -1998, all references to STP assume RSTP unless otherwise indicated.

STP ensures that there is only one logical path between all destinations on the network by intentionally blocking redundant paths that could cause a _____ . A switch port is considered _____ when network traffic is prevented from entering or leaving that port.

STP uses the _____ (STA) to determine which switch ports on a network need to be _____ to prevent _____ from occurring. The STA designates a single switch as the _____ bridge and uses it as the reference point for all subsequent calculations. Switches participating in STP determine which switch has the lowest _____ (BID) on the network. This switch automatically becomes the _____ bridge.

A _____ (BPDU) is a frame containing STP information exchanged by switches running STP. Each BPDU contains a BID that identifies the switch that sent the BPDU. The _____ BID value determines which switch is root.

After the root bridge has been determined, the STA calculates the shortest path to the root bridge. If there is more than one path to choose from, STA chooses the path with the lowest _____ .

When the STA has determined the "best" paths emanating from the root bridge, it configures the switch ports into distinct port roles. The port roles describe their relation in the network to the root bridge and whether they are allowed to forward traffic:

- _____ **ports:** Switch ports closest to the root bridge

- _____ **ports:** Nonroot ports that are still permitted to forward traffic on the network

- _____ **ports:** Ports in a blocking state to prevent loops

- _____ **port:** Ports that are administratively shut down

After a switch boots, it sends BPDU frames containing the switch BID and the root ID every _ seconds. Initially, each switch identifies itself as the ____ bridge after boot.

How would a switch determine that another switch is now the root bridge?

How does the STA determine path cost?

Record the default port costs for various link speeds in Table 2-1.

Table 2-1   Port Costs

Link Speed	Cost (Revised IEEE Specification)	Cost (Previous IEEE Specification)
10 Gbps		
1 Gbps		
100 Mbps		
10 Mbps		

Although switch ports have a default port cost associated with them, the port cost is configurable.

To configure the port cost of an interface, enter the _____ command in interface configuration mode. The range value can be between _____ and _____ .

Record the commands, including the switch prompt, to configure the port cost for F0/1 as 15:

To verify the port and path cost to the root bridge, enter the _____ privileged EXEC mode command, as shown here:

```
S2# _____
```

```
VLAN0001
  Spanning tree enabled protocol ieee
  Root ID    Priority    32769
             Address     c025.5cd7.ef00
             Cost        15
             Port        1 (FastEthernet0/1)
             Hello Time   2 sec  Max Age 20 sec  Forward Delay 15 sec

  Bridge ID  Priority    32769  (priority 32768 sys-id-ext 1)
             Address     c07b.bcc4.a980
             Hello Time   2 sec  Max Age 20 sec  Forward Delay 15 sec
             Aging Time  15  sec

Interface        Role Sts Cost      Prio.Nbr Type
---------------- ---- --- --------- -------- --------------------------------
Fa0/1            Root FWD 15        128.1    P2p
Fa0/2            Altn BLK 19        128.2    P2p
Fa0/3            Desg LIS 19        128.3    P2p
Fa0/4            Desg LIS 19        128.4    P2p
Fa0/6            Desg FWD 19        128.6    P2p<output omitted>
```

The BID field of a BPDU frame contains three separate fields: _____ , _____ , and _____ .

Of these three fields, the _____ is a customizable value that you can use to influence which switch becomes the root bridge. The default value for this field is _____ .

Cisco enhanced its implementation of STP to include support for the extended system ID field, which contains the ID of the _____ with which the BPDU is associated.

Because using the extended system ID changes the number of bits available for the bridge priority, the customizable values can only be multiples of _____ .

When two switches are configured with the same priority and have the same extended system ID, the switch with the lowest _____ has the lower BID.

Identify the 802.1D Port Roles

The topologies in the next three figures do not necessarily represent an appropriate network design. However, they provide good exercise topologies for you to practice determining the STP port roles. In Figures 2-2 through 2-4, use the priority values and MAC addresses to determine the root bridge. Then label the ports with one of the following:

- RP: Root Port

- DP: Designated Port

- AP: Alternate Port

Figure 2-2   802.1D Port Roles - Scenario 1

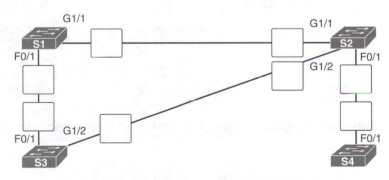

Device	Priority	MAC Address
S1	32769	000a:0001:1111
S2	24577	000a:0002:2222
S3	32769	000a:0003:3333
S4	32769	000a:0004:4444

Figure 2-3   802.1D Port Roles - Scenario 2

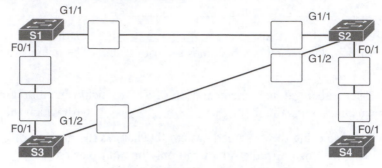

Device	Priority	MAC Address
S1	24577	000a:0001:1111
S2	32769	000a:0002:2222
S3	32769	000a:0003:3333
S4	32769	000a:0004:4444

Figure 2-4   802.1D Port Roles - Scenario 3

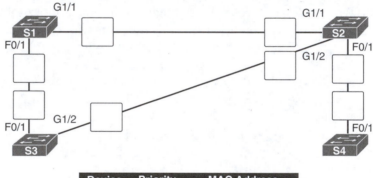

Device	Priority	MAC Address
S1	32769	000a:0001:1111
S2	32769	000a:0002:2222
S3	24577	000a:0003:3333
S4	32769	000a:0004:4444

 Lab – Building a Switched Network with Redundant Links (SN 2.1.2.10/SwN 4.1.2.10)

Varieties of Spanning Tree Protocols

STP has been improved multiple times since its introduction in the original IEEE 802.1D speci-fication. A network administrator should know which type to implement based on the equip-ment and topology needs.

Comparing the STP Varieties

Identify each of the STP varieties described in the following list:

- _____ : This is an IEEE that maps multiple VLANs into the same spanning tree instance.

- _____ : This is an evolution of STP that provides faster conver-gence than STP.

- _____ : This is an updated version of the STP standard, incorporating IEEE 802.1w.

- _____ : This is a Cisco enhancement of STP that provides a separate 802.1D spanning tree instance for each VLAN configured in the network.

- _____ : This is a Cisco enhancement that provides a separate instance of 802.1w per VLAN.

- _____ : This is the original IEEE 802.1D version (802.1D-1998 and earlier) that provides a loop-free topology in a network with redundant links.

Complete the cells in Table 2-2 to identify each the characteristics of each STP variety.

Table 2-2   STP Characteristics - Exercise 1

Protocol	Standard	Resources Needed	Convergence	Tree Calculation
STP		Low		
	Cisco			
	802.1w			
Rapid PVST+				
	802.1s, Cisco	Medium or high		

In Table 2-3, indicate which varieties of STP are best described by the characteristic. Some characteristics apply to more than one STP variety.

Table 2-3   STP Characteristics - Exercise 2

Characteristic	STP	PVST+	RSTP	Rapid PVST+	MSTP	MST
A Cisco implementation of 802.1s that provides up to 16 instances of RSTP.						
Cisco enhancement of RSTP.						
The default STP mode for Cisco Catalyst switches.						
Has the highest CPU and memory requirements.						
Can lead to suboptimal traffic flows.						
Cisco proprietary versions of STP.						
Cisco enhancement of STP. Provides a separate 802.1D spanning-tree instance for each VLAN.						
There is only 1 root bridge and 1 tree.						
Uses 1 IEEE 802.1D spanning-tree instance for the entire bridged network, regardless of the number of VLANs.						
Supports PortFast, BPDU guard, BPDU filter, root guard, and loop guard.						
An evolution of STP that provides faster STP convergence.						

Characteristic	STP	PVST+	RSTP	Rapid PVST+	MSTP	MST
Maps multiple VLANs that have the same traffic flow requirements into the same spanning-tree instance.						
First version of STP to address convergence issues, but still provided only one STP instance.						

PVST+ Operation

After a switch boots, the spanning tree is immediately determined as ports transition through five possible states and three BPDU timers on the way to convergence. Briefly describe each state:

- Blocking:

- Listening:

- Learning:

- Forwarding:

- Disabled:

Once stable, every active port in the switched network is either in the _____ state or the _____ state.

List and briefly describe the four steps PVST+ performs for each VLAN to provide a loop-free logical topology.

In Table 2-4, answer the "Operation Allowed" question with "yes" or "no" for each port state.

Table 2-4   Operations Allowed at Each Port State

Operation Allowed	Port State				
	Blocking	Listening	Learning	Forwarding	Disabled
Can receive and process BPDUs					
Can forward data frames received on interface					
Can forward data frames switched from another interface					
Can learn MAC addresses					

Rapid PVST+ Operation

RSTP (IEEE _____) is an evolution of the original _____ standard and is incorporated into the IEEE _____ -2004 standard. Rapid PVST+ is the Cisco implementation of RSTP on a per-VLAN basis. What is the primary difference between Rapid PVST+ and RSTP?

Briefly describe the RSTP concept that corresponds to the PVST+ PortFast feature.

What command implements Cisco's version of an edge port?

In Table 2-5, indicate whether the characteristic describes PVST+, Rapid PVST+, or both.

Table 2-5   Comparing PVST+ and Rapid PVST+

Characteristic	PVST+	Rapid PVST+	Both
Cisco proprietary protocol.			
Port roles: root, designated, alternate, edge, backup.			
CPU processing and trunk bandwidth usage is greater than with STP.			
Ports can transition to forwarding state without relying on a timer.			
The root bridge is determined by the lowest BID + VLAN ID + MAC.			
Runs a separate IEEE 802.1D STP instance for each VLAN.			
Possible to have load sharing with some VLANS forwarding on each trunk.			
Sends a BPDU "hello message" every 2 seconds.			

Spanning-Tree Configuration

It is crucial to understand the impact of a default switch configuration on STP convergence and what configurations can be applied to adjust the default behavior.

PVST+ and Rapid PVST+ Configuration

Complete Table 2-6 to show the default spanning-tree configuration for a Cisco Catalyst 2960 series switch.

Table 2-6   Default Switch Configuration

Feature	Default Setting
Enable state	Enabled on VLAN 1
Spanning-tree mode	
Switch priority	
Spanning-tree port priority (configurable on a per-interface basis)	
Spanning-tree port cost (configurable on a per-interface basis)	1000 Mbps:
	100 Mbps:
	10 Mbps:
Spanning-tree VLAN port priority (configurable on a per-VLAN basis)	
Spanning-tree VLAN port cost (configurable on a per-VLAN basis)	1000 Mbps:
	100 Mbps:
	10 Mbps:
Spanning-tree timers	Hello time: seconds
	Forward-delay time: seconds
	Maximum-aging time: seconds
	Transmit hold count: BPDUs

Document the two different configuration commands that you can use to configure the bridge priority value so that the switch is root for VLAN 1. Use the value 4096 when necessary:

Record the command to verify that the local switch is now root:

```
S1# _____


VLAN0001
  Spanning tree enabled protocol ieee
  Root ID    Priority    24577
             Address     000A.0033.3333
             This bridge is the root
             Hello Time   2 sec  Max Age 20 sec  Forward Delay 15 sec
```

```
    Bridge ID   Priority    24577   (priority 24576 sys-id-ext 1)
                Address     0019.aa9e.b000
                Hello Time   2 sec  Max Age 20 sec  Forward Delay 15 sec
                Aging Time 300


Interface          Role Sts Cost      Prio.Nbr Type
---------------- ---- --- --------- -------- -------------------------------
Fa0/1              Desg FWD 4         128.1    Shr
Fa0/2              Desg FWD 4         128.2    Shr
```

Explain the purpose of the BPDU guard feature on Cisco switches.

What command interface configuration command enables BPDU guard?

What global configuration command will configure all nontrunking ports as edge ports?

What global configuration command will configure BPDU guard on all PortFast-enabled ports?

The power of PVST+ is that it can load balance across redundant links. By default, the least-favored redundant link is not used. So, you must manually configure PVST+ to use the link.

Figure 2-5 represents a small section of Figure 2-1, showing only two distribution layer switches and one access layer switch. For this example, we have attached PC2 to S1. PC1 is assigned to VLAN 15, and PC2 is assigned to VLAN 25. D1 should be the primary root for VLAN 1 and VLAN 15 and the secondary root for VLAN 25. D2 should be the primary root for VLAN 25 and the secondary root for VLAN 15.

Figure 2-5   PVST+ Configuration Topology

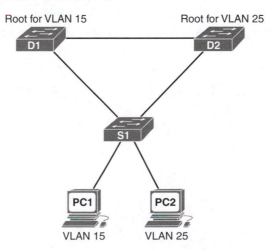

Based on these requirements, document the commands to modify the default PVST+ operation on D1 and D2.

D1 commands

D2 commands

Document the commands to configure all nontrunking ports on S1 as edge ports with BPDU guard enabled.

Now, assume that you want to run rapid PVST+ on all three switches. What command is required?

Lab - Configuring Rapid PVST+, PortFast, and BPDU Guard (SN 2.3.2.3/SwN 4.3.2.3)

Packet Tracer - Configuring PVST+ (SN 2.3.1.5/SwN 4.3.1.5)

Packet Tracer - Configuring Rapid PVST+ (SN 2.3.2.2/SwN 4.3.2.2)

First Hop Redundancy Protocols

Up to this point, we've been reviewing STP and how to manipulate the election of root bridges and load balance across redundant links. In addition to Layer 1 and Layer 2 redundancy, a high-availability network might also implement Layer 3 redundancy by sharing the default gateway responsibility across multiple devices. Through the use of a virtual IP address, two Layer 3 devices can share the default gateway responsibility. The section reviews First Hop Redundancy Protocols (FHRPs) that provide Layer 3 redundancy.

Identify FHRP Terminology

Match the definition on the left with the terms on the right. This is a one-to-one matching exercise.

Definitions

_____ The ability to dynamically recover from the failure of a device acting as the default gateway

_____ Two or more routers sharing a single MAC and IP address

_____ A device that is part of a virtual router group assigned to the role of default gateway

_____ Provides the mechanism for determining which router should take the active role in forwarding traffic

_____ A device that routes traffic destined to network segments beyond the source network segment

_____ A device that is part of a virtual router group assigned the role of alternate default gateway

_____ A Layer 3 address assigned to a protocol that shares the single address among multiple devices

_____ The Layer 2 address returned by ARP for an FHRP gateway

Terms

a. Default gateway

b. First-hop redundancy

c. Forwarding router

d. Redundancy rrotocol

e. Standby router

f. Virtual IP address

g. Virtual MAC address

h. Virtual router

Identify the Type of FHRP

In Table 2-7, indicate whether the characteristic describes HSRP, VRRP, or GLBP.

Table 2-7   FHRP Characteristics

FHRP Characteristic	HSRP	VRRP	GLBP
Used in a group of routers for selecting an active device and a stand-by device.			
A nonproprietary election protocol that allows several routers on a multi-access link to use the same virtual IPv4 address.			
Cisco-proprietary FHRP protocol designed to allow for transparent failover of a first-hop IPv4 devices.			
Cisco-proprietary FHRP protocol that protects data traffic from a failed router or circuit while also allowing load sharing between a group of redundant routers.			
One router is elected as the virtual router master, with the other routers acting as backups in case the virtual router master fails.			

HSRP and GLBP Configuration and Verification

Refer to the topology in Figure 2-6. R2 has been configured for HSRP group 20, priority 120, IP address 192.168.1.20, and virtual IP address 192.168.1.1.

Figure 2-6   HSRP and GLBP Configuration Topology

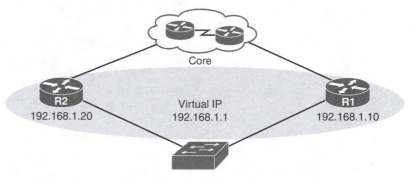

Example 2-1 shows the HSRP configuration for R2.

Example 2-1   R2 HSRP Configuration

```
R2# show run interface g0/1
<output omitted>
interface GigabitEthernet0/1
 ip address 192.168.1.20 255.255.255.0
 standby 20 ip 192.168.1.1
 standby 20 priority 120
<output omitted>
```

Using the information in Example 2-1, document the commands to configure R1 as the HSRP active router in group 20 using a priority of 210.

What command would generate the following output to verify the HSRP configuration?

```
R1#_____

                    P indicates configured to preempt.

                    |

Interface   Grp  Pri P State   Active         Standby        Virtual IP
Gi0/1       20   210   Active  local          192.168.1.20   192.168.1.1
```

Now assume that all HSRP configurations have been removed. R2 has been configured for GLBP group 20, priority 120, IP address 192.168.1.20, and virtual IP address 192.168.1.1.

Example 2-2 shows the GLBP configuration for R2.

Example 2-2   R2 GLBP Configuration

```
R2# show run interface g0/1
<output omitted>
interface GigabitEthernet0/1
 ip address 192.168.1.20 255.255.255.0
 glbp 20 ip 192.168.1.1
 glbp 20 priority 120
<output omitted>
```

Using the information in Example 2-2, document the commands to configure R1 to be in GLBP group 20 using a priority of 210.

What command would generate the following output to verify the GLBP configuration?

```
R1#_____
GigabitEthernet0/0 - Group 20
  State is Active
    1 state change, last state change 00:03:05
  Virtual IP address is 192.168.1.1
```

```
Hello time 3 sec, hold time 10 sec
  Next hello sent in 1.792 secs
Redirect time 600 sec, forwarder timeout 14400 sec
Preemption disabled
Active is local
Standby is 192.168.1.20, priority 120 (expires in 9.024 sec)
Priority 210 (configured)
Weighting 100 (default 100), thresholds: lower 1, upper 100
Load balancing: round-robin
Group members:
  0006.f671.db58 (192.168.1.10) local
  0006.f671.eb38 (192.168.1.20)
There are 2 forwarders (1 active)
Forwarder 1
  State is Active
    1 state change, last state change 00:02:53
  MAC address is 0007.b400.0a01 (default)
  Owner ID is 0006.f671.db58
  Redirection enabled
  Preemption enabled, min delay 30 sec
  Active is local, weighting 100
Forwarder 2
  State is Listen
  MAC address is 0007.b400.0a02 (learnt)
  Owner ID is 0006.f671.eb38
  Redirection enabled, 599.040 sec remaining (maximum 600 sec)
  Time to live: 14399.040 sec (maximum 14400 sec)
  Preemption enabled, min delay 30 sec
  Active is 192.168.1.20 (primary), weighting 100 (expires in 9.312 sec)
```

 Lab - Configuring HSRP and GLBP (SN 2.4.3.4/SwN 4.4.3.4)

CHAPTER 3

Link Aggregation

Link aggregation is the ability to create one logical link using multiple physical links between two devices. This allows load sharing among the physical links, rather than having a STP block one or more of the links.

Link Aggregation Concepts

One of the best ways to reduce the time it takes for STP convergence is to simply avoid STP. EtherChannel is a form of link aggregation used in switched networks.

EtherChannel Advantages

EtherChannel technology was originally developed by Cisco as a technique of grouping several Fast Ethernet or Gigabit Ethernet switch ports into one logical channel.

List at least three advantages to using EtherChannel:

-

-

-

-

-

EtherChannel Operation

You can configure EtherChannel as static or unconditional. However, there are also two protocols that can be used to configure the negotiation process: Port Aggregation Protocol (PAgP—Cisco proprietary) and Link Aggregation Control Protocol (LACP—IEEE 802.3ad).

These two protocols ensure that both sides of the link have compatible configurations—same speed, duplex setting, and VLAN information. The modes for each differ slightly.

For PAgP, briefly describe each of the following modes:

- **On:**
- **Desirable:**
- **Auto:**

For LACP, briefly describe each of the following modes:

- **On:**
- **Active:**
- **Passive:**

In Table 3-1, indicate the mode that is described.

Table 3-1   PAgP and LACP Modes

Mode	PAgP and/or LACP Mode Description
	Initiates LACP negotiations with other interfaces.
	Forces EtherChannel state without PAgP or LACP initiated negotiations.
	Places an interface in a passive, responding state. Does not initiate PAgP negotiations.
	Actively initiates PAgP negotiations with other interfaces.
	Places an interface in a passive, responding state. Does not initiate LACP negotiations.

The mode that is configured on each side of the EtherChannel link determines whether EtherChannel will be operational.

In Table 3-2, two switches are using PAgP. Indicate with "yes" or "no" whether EtherChannel is established.

Table 3-2   EtherChannel Negotiation Using PAgP

Switch 1 Mode	Switch 2 Mode	EtherChannel Established?
Auto	Auto	
Auto	Desirable	
On	Desirable	
On	Off	
Desirable	Desirable	

In Table 3-3, two switches are using LACP. Indicate with "yes" or "no" whether EtherChannel is established.

Table 3-3   EtherChannel Negotiation Using LACP

Switch 1 Mode	Switch 2 Mode	EtherChannel Established?
Passive	On	
Passive	Active	
On	On	
Passive	Passive	
On	Active	

Link Aggregation Configuration

EtherChannel configuration is rather straightforward once you decide on which protocol you will use. In fact, the easiest method is to just force both sides to be on.

Configuring EtherChannel

To configure EtherChannel, complete the following steps:

Step 1. Specify the interfaces that, participate in the EtherChannel group using the **interface range** *interface* command.

What are the requirements for each interface before they can form an EtherChannel?

Step 2. Create the port channel interface with the **channel-group** *identifier* **mode** {**on** | **auto** | **desirable** | **active** | **passive**} command in interface range configuration mode. The keyword _____ forces the port to channel without PAgP or LACP. The keywords _____ and _____ enable PAgP. The keywords _____ and _____ enable LACP.

Step 3. The **channel-group** command automatically creates a port channel interface using the *identifier* as the number. Use the **interface port-channel** *identifier* command to configure channel-wide settings like trunking, native VLANs, or allowed VLANs.

As you can see from the configuration steps, the way you specify whether to use PAgP, LACP, or no negotiations is by configuring one keyword in the **channel-group** command.

So, with those steps in mind, consider Figure 3-1 in each of the following configuration scenarios.

Figure 3-1   EtherChannel Topology

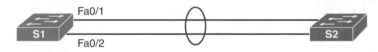

EtherChannel Configuration Scenario 1

Record the commands, including the switch prompt, to configure the S1 Fa0/1 and Fa0/2 into an EtherChannel without negotiations. Then force the channel to trunking using native VLAN 99.

```
S1(config)#
```


EtherChannel Configuration Scenario 1

Record the commands, including the switch prompt, to configure the S1 Fa0/1 and Fa0/2 into an EtherChannel using PAgP. S1 should initiate the negotiations. The channel should trunk, allowing only VLANs 1, 10, and 20.

```
S1(config)#
```

EtherChannel Configuration Scenario 1

Record the commands, including the switch prompt, to configure the S1 Fa0/1 and Fa0/2 into an EtherChannel using LACP. S1 should not initiate the negotiations. The channel should trunk, allowing all VLANs.

```
S1(config)#
```

Lab - Configuring EtherChannel (SN 3.2.1.4/SwN 5.2.1.4)

Packet Tracer - Configuring EtherChannel (SN 3.2.1.3/SwN 5.2.1.3)

Verifying and Troubleshooting EtherChannel

Record the commands used to display the output in Example 3-1.

Example 3-1   EtherChannel Verification Commands

```
S1# _____

Port-channel1 is up, line protocol is up (connected)
  Hardware is EtherChannel, address is 0cd9.96e8.8a01 (bia 0cd9.96e8.8a01)
  MTU 1500 bytes, BW 200000 Kbit/sec, DLY 100 usec,
     reliability 255/255, txload 1/255, rxload 1/255
<output omitted>


S1# _____

Flags:  D - down        P - bundled in port-channel
        I - stand-alone s - suspended
        H - Hot-standby (LACP only)
        R - Layer3       S - Layer2
        U - in use       f - failed to allocate aggregator

        M - not in use, minimum links not met
        u - unsuitable for bundling
        w - waiting to be aggregated
        d - default port



Number of channel-groups in use: 1
Number of aggregators:           1
```

```
Group   Port-channel  Protocol    Ports
------+-------------+-----------+-----------------------------------------------
1       Po1(SU)       LACP        Fa0/1(P)    Fa0/2(P)


S1# _____
                Channel-group listing:
                ----------------------


Group: 1
----------
                Port-channels in the group:
                ---------------------------


Port-channel: Po1    (Primary Aggregator)


------------


Age of the Port-channel   = 0d:00h:25m:17s
Logical slot/port   = 2/1          Number of ports = 2
HotStandBy port = null
Port state          = Port-channel Ag-Inuse
Protocol            =   LACP
Port security       = Disabled


Ports in the Port-channel:


Index   Load   Port    EC state          No of bits
------+------+------+------------------+-----------
  0     00     Fa0/1   Active                0
  0     00     Fa0/2   Active                0


Time since last port bundled:    0d:00h:05m:41s    Fa0/2
Time since last port Un-bundled: 0d:00h:05m:48s    Fa0/2


S1# _____
Port state     = Up Mstr Assoc In-Bndl
Channel group = 1            Mode = Active        Gcchange = -
Port-channel = Po1           GC   = -             Pseudo port-channel = Po1
Port index   = 0             Load = 0x00          Protocol =   LACP


Flags:  S - Device is sending Slow LACPDUs   F - Device is sending fast LACPDUs.
        A - Device is in active mode.         P - Device is in passive mode.
```

```
Local information:

                              LACP port   Admin    Oper    Port      Port
Port        Flags   State     Priority    Key      Key     Number    State
Fa0/1       SA      bndl      32768       0x1      0x1     0x102     0x3D


Partner's information:

                    LACP port                     Admin   Oper   Port     Port
Port        Flags   Priority   Dev ID        Age   key     Key    Number   State
Fa0/1       SA      32768      0cd9.96d2.4000 4s   0x0     0x1    0x102    0x3D


Age of the port in the current state: 0d:00h:24m:59s
S1#
```

When troubleshooting an EtherChannel issue, keep in mind the configuration restrictions for interfaces that participate in the channel. List at least four restrictions.

-
-
-
-
-

Refer to the output for S1 and S2 in Example 3-2. Record the command that generated the output.

Example 3-2   Troubleshooting an EtherChannel Issue

```
S1# _____

Flags:  D - down          P - bundled in port-channel

        I - stand-alone s - suspended

        H - Hot-standby (LACP only)

        R - Layer3        S - Layer2

        U - in use        f - failed to allocate aggregator

        M - not in use, minimum links not met

        u - unsuitable for bundling

        w - waiting to be aggregated

        d - default port

Number of channel-groups in use: 1

Number of aggregators:          1

Group  Port-channel  Protocol    Ports

------+-------------+-----------+-----------------------------------------------

1      Po1(SD)          -        Fa0/1(D)     Fa0/2(D)
S1# show run | begin interface Port-channel
```

```
interface Port-channel1
 switchport mode trunk
!
interface FastEthernet0/1
 switchport mode trunk
 channel-group 1 mode auto
!
interface FastEthernet0/2
 switchport mode trunk
 channel-group 1 mode auto
!
<output omitted>
S 1#
```

```
S2# show run | begin interface Port-channel
interface Port-channel1
 switchport mode trunk
!
interface FastEthernet0/1
 switchport mode trunk
 channel-group 1 mode auto
!
interface FastEthernet0/2
 switchport mode trunk
 channel-group 1 mode auto
!
<output omitted>
S2#
```

Explain why the EtherChannel between S1 and S2 is down.

EtherChannel and spanning tree must interoperate. For this reason, the order in which EtherChannel-related commands are entered is important. To correct this issue, you must first remove the port channel. Otherwise, spanning-tree errors cause the associated ports to go into blocking or errdisabled state. With that in mind, what would you suggest to correct the issue shown in Example 3-2 if the requirement is to use PAgP? What commands would be required?

Lab - Troubleshooting EtherChannel (SN 3.2.2.4/SwN 5.2.2.4)

Packet Tracer
☐ Activity

Packet Tracer - Troubleshooting EtherChannel (SN 3.2.2.3/SwN 5.2.2.3)

Packet Tracer - Skills Integration Challenge (SN 3.3.1.2/SwN 5.3.1.2)

CHAPTER 4

Wireless LANs

Wireless networks are becoming increasingly ubiquitous. If you have a router at home, chances are it supports a wireless LAN (WLAN). In the work environment, WLANs provide the ability to connect from any location at any time within the campus network. WLANs use radio frequencies that present some unique design and implementation considerations. This chapter reviews WLAN technology, components, security, planning, implementation, and troubleshooting.

Wireless LAN Concepts

Wireless access can result in increased productivity and more relaxed employees. With wireless networking, employees have the flexibility to work when they want, where they want. This section reviews basic wireless concepts and components.

Identify Wireless Technologies

When referring to communication networks, the term *wireless* encompasses a wide variety of technologies. Although the focus for the CCNA student is on WLANs, you should also be aware of the basic features of other wireless technologies and applications. In Table 4-1, indicate the wireless technology described by each feature.

Table 4-1   Identify the Wireless Technology

Wireless Technology Feature	Bluetooth	Wi-Fi	WiMax	Cellular	Satellite
Clear line of sight required					
IEEE 802.16					
IEEE 802.15					
Uses 2G, 3G, and 4G variations					
Supports speeds up to 1 Gbps					
Provides mobile broadband connectivity					
Supports download speeds up to 10 Mbps					
Supports speeds up to 5 Mbps					
Distance transmissions of up to 300 meters					
Requires directional dish aligned with GEO device					
Supports speeds up to 24 Mbps					
Transmission distances of up to 30 miles (50 km)					
Distance transmissions of up to 100 meters					
Supports speeds up to 7 Gbps					
IEEE 802.11					

WLANs standards began in 1997 with the first 802.11 specification. Subsequent revisions have increased the speed and changed the frequency. As the standard rapidly evolved, it became important to maintain backward compatibility so that devices would still be able to connect to newer and faster access points.

In Table 4-2, all the current flavors of 802.11 are listed in chronological order. For each one, indicate the maximum speed, frequency or frequencies, and with what earlier versions the specification is compatible (if any).

Table 4-2   Comparing the WLAN Standards

IEEE Standard	Maximum Speed	Frequency	Backward Compatibility With
802.11			
802.11a			
802.11b			
802.11g			
802.11n			
802.11ac			
802.11ad			

Using your completed Table 4-2, indicate in Table 4-3 the frequencies at which each standard operates.

Table 4-3   WLAN Standards and Frequencies

2.4 GHz (UHF)	5 GHz (SFH)	60 GHz (EHF)
802.11a	802.11a	802.11a
802.11b	802.11b	802.11b
802.11g	802.11g	802.11g
802.11n	802.11n	802.11n
802.11ac	802.11ac	802.11ac
802.11ad	802.11ad	802.11ad

As a network technician, you should be aware of other wireless applications that could potentially cause problems with your WLAN implementations. In Table 4-4, indicate the frequency for each wireless application. Some applications may use more than one frequency.

Table 4-4   Wireless Application Frequencies

Wireless Application	2.4 GHz (UHF)	5 GHz (SHF)	60 GHz (EHF)
Cellular broadband			
Radar landing systems			
GPS systems			
Radio astronomy			
Bluetooth			
Satellite communications			
Microwave communications			

In Table 4-5, indicate whether the feature describes LANs or WLANs.

Table 4-5   Comparing LANs and WLANs

WLAN or LAN Feature	802.3 LANs	802.11 WLANs
Collision detection (CSMA/CD).		
Cables are used to interconnect devices.		
Additional laws and regulations in local areas may apply.		
Allows for device mobility.		
Signal interference is normally not a problem.		
Collision avoidance (CSMA/CA).		
Connects to an Ethernet switch.		
Radio frequencies (RFs) are used to interconnect devices.		
Connects to an access point.		
Provides for better security.		

WLANs Components and Topologies

Today, all laptops, tablets, and smartphones include an integrated wireless NIC. However, desktop computers usually do not. In a home or small office network, it might not be desirable or feasible to run cabling to a desktop. In such situations, you can easily install a wireless network interface card (NIC) to provide connectivity.

Wireless NICs associate (and possibly authenticate) with an access point (AP). Briefly explain the difference between an autonomous AP and controller-based AP.

Two or more autonomous APs can be combined into a cluster to ease management requirements. What four conditions must be met before a cluster can be formed:

-
-
-
-

Briefly explain the two main 802.11 wireless topologies:

- **Ad hoc mode:**

- **Infrastructure mode:**

In Figure 4-1, label the two wireless topologies with either infrastructure mode or ad hoc mode.

Figure 4-1   WLAN Topologies

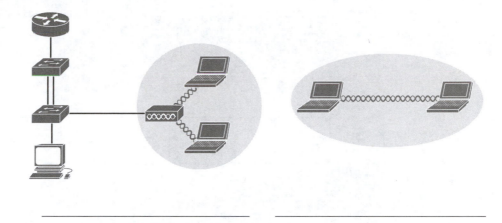

_____   _____

Infrastructure mode uses two topology building blocks: a basic service set (BSS) and an extended service set (ESS). Briefly describe each and how they interrelate.

 Lab - Investigating Wireless Implementations (SN 4.1.2.10/SwN 8.1.2.10)

Wireless LAN Operations

WLAN operations have similar structures and concepts to Ethernet's 802.3. 802.11 uses a frame format similar to 802.3, but with more fields. 802.11 uses a collision detection system similar to Ethernet's carrier sense multiple access collision detect (CSMA/CD). However, Ethernet does not have to worry about finding, authenticating, and associating with an AP. Nor does Ethernet have to worry about managing channels on the wireless radio frequencies. This section reviews the 802.11 frame, CSMA/CA, AP association, and channel management.

Label the 802.11 Frame

In Figure 4-2, label each field in the 802.11 frame.

Figure 4-2   802.11 Frame Format

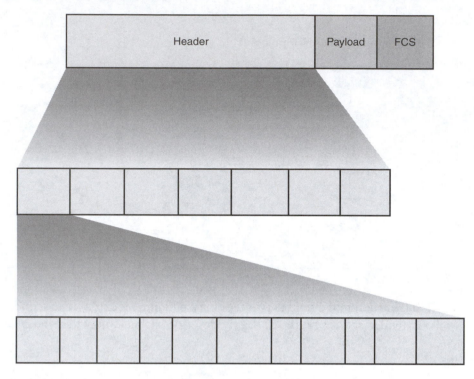

Match the subfield description on the left with the subfield on the right. This is a one-to-one matching exercise.

Subfield Description

_____ Indicates whether encryption/authentication is being used

_____ Identifies the frame as either a management, control, or data frame

_____ Active or power-save mode status of the sending device

_____ Specifies which 802.11 protocols is being used

_____ Indicates to an associated AP client that data is exiting a DS (distributed system)

Subfield

a. Protocol version

b. Frame subtype

c. FromDS

d. Power management

e. Security

Wireless Media Contention

A wireless device operates in a half-duplex, shared media environment. So, a wireless device must also sense the carrier because multiple devices have access—carrier sense multiple access (CSMA). However, unlike half-duplex Ethernet operations, a wireless device that is sending cannot also listen for collision. Therefore, IEEE developed a collision avoidance (the CA in CSMA/CA) mechanism called the distributed coordination function (DCF). Using DCF, a wireless client transmits only if the channel is clear. All transmissions are acknowledged. Therefore, if a wireless client does not receive an acknowledgment, it assumes a collision occurred and retries after a random waiting interval. In the flowchart in Figure 4-3, label the missing steps in the CSMA/CA process.

Figure 4-3   CSMA/CA Process

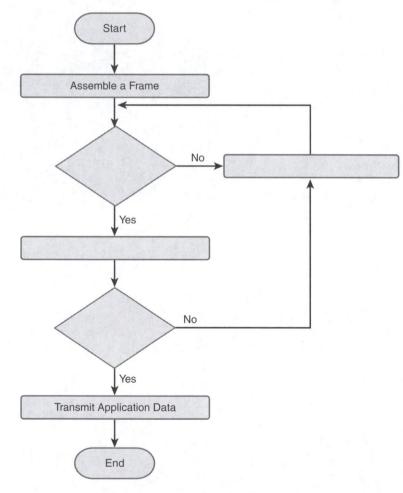

Associating with an AP

Before a wireless device can communicate over the network, it must first associate with an AP or wireless router. To do so, it must discover and authenticate with an AP.

Match the definitions on the left with the association parameter on the right. This is a one-to-one matching activity.

Definitions

_____ A unique identifier that wireless clients use to distinguish between multiple wireless networks in the same vicinity

_____ Identifies the 802.11 WLAN standards supported by the AP

_____ Currently standards include WEP, WPA, or WPA2

_____ Refers to the frequency bands being used to transmit wireless data

_____ Prevents intruders and other unwanted users from associating with the AP

Security Parameter

a. Security mode

b. Password

c. Channel settings

d. Network mode

e. SSID

To discover and connect with an AP or wireless routers, clients use a probing process, which can either be passive or active, as shown in Figure 4-4. Label each example as either passive or active.

Figure 4-4   Two Methods to Discover an AP

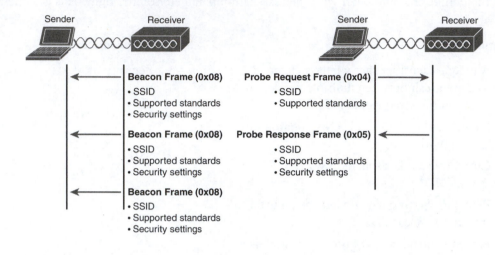

Briefly explain the two authentication mechanisms:

- **Open authentication:**

- **Shared-key authentication:**

After discovering and authenticating with an AP or wireless router, the wireless device goes through an association process. Label Step 3 in Figure 4-5 with the association substeps.

Figure 4-5   The AP Association Process

Channel Management Concepts

In wireless implementations, a common practice is for the radio wave frequencies to be allocated as ranges. Such ranges are then split into smaller ranges called channels. Depending on the 802.11 standard, there are various ways to manage these channels. Match the channels, frequency modulation technique, or standard on the right with the definitions on the left.

Definitions

_____ Spreads the signal over larger-frequency bands; used by 802.11b, cordless phones, CDMA cellular, and GPS networks

_____ Number of channels identified in Europe for 802.11b

_____ Nonoverlapping 802.11b channels

_____ Rapidly switches the signal over many frequency channels; used by the original 802.11 standard, walkie-talkies, and Bluetooth

_____ Supports four nonoverlapping channels and channel bonding

_____ Number of channels identified in North America for 802.11b

_____ Maximizes spectral efficiency without causing adjacent channel interference; used by 802.11a/g/n/ad

Channels, Frequency Modulation, and Standards

a. 11

b. 12

c. 13

d. 1,5,10

e. 1,6,11

f. 802.11g

g. 802.11n

h. DSSS

i. FHSS

j. OFDM

Wireless LAN Security

WLANs present unique security concerns because anyone within range of the AP and with the correct credentials can gain access to the network.

WLAN Security Terminology

Match the definitions on the left with the WLAN security terms on the right. This is a one-to-one matching exercise.

Definitions

_____ Wireless home router connected to the corporate network without authorization

_____ Attacker sends a series of "disassociate" commands to all wireless clients within a BSS

_____ Attacker takes advantage of the CSMA/CA contention method to monopolize the bandwidth and deny all other clients access to the AP

_____ The 802.11i industry standard for securing wireless networks

_____ An AP configured with the same SSID as a legitimate AP

_____ Uses Message Integrity Check (MIC) to ensure the message has not been tampered with

_____ Basically WEP with TKIP encryption

_____ Obsolete wireless authentication method

_____ Manually allow or deny based on physical address

_____ Disable the transmission of the beacon

_____ Uses Counter Mode Cipher Block Chaining Message Authentication Code Protocol (CCMP), which allows destination hosts to recognize whether the bits have been tampered with

WLAN Security Term

a. TKIP

b. Man-in-the-middle attack

c. SSID cloaking

d. AES

e. WEP

f. Spoofed disconnect attack

g. CTS Flood

h. WPA

i. MAC address filtering

j. WPA2

k. Rogue AP

Identify the WLAN Security Characteristics

The best way to secure a wireless network is to use authentication and encryption systems. The two major types of authentication are open authentication and shared authentication. Open is basically no authentication. Shared-key authentication comes in three flavors: WEP, WPA, and WPA2. In Table 4-6, indicate the authentication method for each characteristic.

Table 4-6   WLAN Security Characteristics

WLAN Security Characteristic	Open Authentication	Shared-Key Authentication		
		WEP	WPA	WPA2
TKIP data encryption				
AES data encryption				
MIC authentication				
No password authentication				
Medium security risk				
Shared-key authentication				
RC4 data encryption				
No data encryption				
Highest security risk				
Lowest security risk				
High security risk				
CCMP authentication				

Wireless LAN Configuration

Modern wireless routers offer a variety of features, and most are designed to be functional right out of the box with the default settings. However, it is good practice to change this initial configuration—particularly, the default administrator password—so that public known default settings cannot be used to access the wireless settings.

Configuring WLAN Routers and Clients

The best way to practice configuring wireless routers is to complete the Lab and Packet Tracer activities associated with the course. You can also make sure your own home router is configured with some of the following settings:

- Change the administrator password.

- Change the IP addressing assigned through DHCP to wireless clients.

- Change the service set identification (SSID) name. However, if you disable SSID broadcasts, users will have to manually enter the SSID.

- Enable the strongest authentication protocol supported by the wireless router: hopefully WPA2.

- Enable MAC address filtering if you know the devices that will be joining the WLAN. Otherwise, you will have to manually add new devices each time someone wants to access the WLAN.

- If desired, configure a guest network and password for guest users to access the WLAN.

If you do not have access to a wireless router, Packet Tracer, or Lab equipment, you can search the Internet for "wireless router configuration simulation." Several wireless router manufacturers host a simulation web page where you can practice configuring their specific GUI.

 Lab - Configuring a Wireless Router and Client (SN 4.4.2.3/SwN 8.4.2.3)

Packet Tracer - Configuring Wireless LAN Access (SN 4.4.2.2/SwN 8.4.2.2)

Packet Tracer
☐ Activity

Troubleshooting WLAN Issues

Troubleshooting WLAN issues normally requires an elimination process. Start with the wireless client by checking the following:

- Does the client have a valid IP address configuration?

- Can the client successfully access the wired network?

- Is the client configured with the correct security settings?

- Is the client configured with the correct channel and SSID?

- Is the wireless NIC driver up-to-date?

If the wireless client is operating as expected, check the following:

- Is the AP powered on?

- How far away is the closest AP?

- Are other devices in the area interfering with the signal?

- Are there any cabling or connector issues?

Finally, check the configuration of the AP to verify that it conforms to the desired specifications.

Occasionally, issues with the AP software are identified and corrected by the manufacturer. So, you should regularly check to make sure that the firmware is up-to-date on the AP.

 Packet Tracer - Skills Integration Challenge (SN 4.5.1.2/SwN 8.5.1.2)

Packet Tracer
☐ Challenge

CHAPTER 5

Adjust and Troubleshoot Single-Area OSPF

Although we will spend a little bit of time on it, you should already know how to configure basic single-area OSPF. This chapter focuses on the concepts and configurations to fine-tune the operation of OSPF, including manipulating the designated router / backup designated router (DR/BDR) election, propagating a default router, fine-tuning Open Shortest Path First (OSPF) Protocol interfaces, and authenticating OSPF neighbors.

Advanced Single-Area OSPF Configurations

In this section, we review the concepts and configurations to fine-tune the operation of OSPFv2 and OSPFv3.

Single-Area OSPF Configuration Review

The following activity may look familiar to you if you also used the *CCENT Practice and Study Guide*. It is repeated here so that you can get back up to speed on OSPF before we look at more advanced configurations.

Configuring Single-Area OSPFv2

Figure 5-1 shows the topology that we will use to configure OSPFv2 and OSPFv3. This first topology shows IPv4 network addresses. The IPv4 addressing scheme is in Table 5-1.

Figure 5-1   OSPFv2 Topology with IPv4 Network Addresses

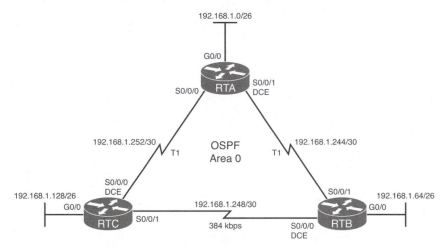

Table 5-1   IPv4 Addressing Scheme for OSPFv2

Device	Interface	IPv4 Address	Subnet Mask
RTA	G0/0	192.168.1.1	255.255.255.192
	S0/0/0	192.168.1.253	255.255.255.252
	S0/0/1	192.168.1.245	255.255.255.252
	Router ID	1.1.1.1	
RTB	G0/0	192.168.1.65	255.255.255.192
	S0/0/0	192.168.1.249	255.255.255.252
	S0/0/1	192.168.1.246	255.255.255.252
	Router ID	2.2.2.2	
RTC	G0/0	192.168.1.129	255.255.255.192
	S0/0/0	192.168.1.254	255.255.255.252
	S0/0/1	192.168.1.250	255.255.255.252
	Router ID	3.3.3.3	

In the space provided, document the correct commands, including the router prompt, to configure the routers in Figure 5-1 with OSPFv2. Include commands to configure the router ID and disable updates on the LAN interface.

Verifying Single-Area OSPFv2

Fill in the missing command to complete the following sentences:

The _____ command can be used to verify and troubleshoot OSPF neighbor relationships.

The _____ command is a quick way to verify vital OSPF configuration information, including the OSPF process ID, the router ID, networks the router is advertising, the neighbors the router is receiving updates from, and the default administrative distance, which is 110 for OSPF.

The _____ command can also be used to examine the OSPF process ID and router ID. In addition, this command displays the OSPF area information as well as the last time the SPF algorithm was calculated.

The quickest way to verify Hello and Dead intervals is to use the _____ command.

The quickest way to verify OSPF convergence is to use the _____ command to view the routing table for each router in the topology.

Configuring Single-Area OSPFv3

Figure 5-2 shows the same topology we used for OSPFv2, but with IPv6 network addresses. Table 5-2 shows the IPv6 addressing scheme.

Figure 5-2   OSPFv3 Topology with IPv6 Network Addresses

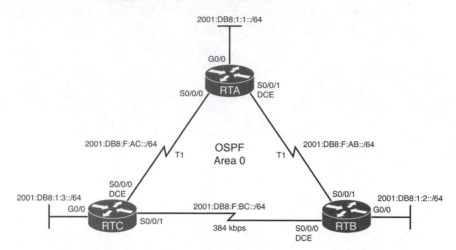

Table 5-2   IPv6 Addressing Scheme for OSPFv3

Device	Interface	IPv6 Address/Prefix
RTA	G0/0	2001:DB8:1:1::1/64
	S0/0/0	2001:DB8:F:AC::1/64
	S0/0/1	2001:DB8:F:AB::1/64
	Link-local	FE80::A
	Router ID	1.1.1.1
RTB	G0/0	2001:DB8:1:2::1/64
	S0/0/0	2001:DB8:F:BC::1/64
	S0/0/1	2001:DB8:F:AB::2/64
	Link-local	FE80::B
	Router ID	2.2.2.2
RTC	G0/0	2001:DB8:1:3::1/64
	S0/0/0	2001:DB8:F:AC::2/64
	S0/0/1	2001:DB8:F:BC::2/64
	Link-local	FE80::C
	Router ID	3.3.3.3

The routers are already configured with interface addressing. Record the correct commands, including the router prompt, to configure the routers with OSPFv3. Include commands to enable IPv6 routing, configure the router ID, change the reference bandwidth to 10000, and disable updates on the LAN interface. Except for the router ID, the commands are the same for all three routers. So, you need to document only one router.

Verifying Single-Area OSPFv3

Fill in the missing command to complete the following sentences:

The _____ command can be used to verify and troubleshoot OSPF neighbor relationships.

The _____ command is a quick way to verify vital OSPF configuration information, including the OSPF process ID, the router ID, and interfaces the router is advertising.

The _____ command can also be used to examine the OSPF process ID and router ID. In addition, this command displays the OSPF area information as well as the last time the SPF algorithm was calculated.

To view a quick summary of OSPFv3-enabled interfaces, use the_____ command. However, the quickest way to verify Hello and Dead intervals is to use the _____ command.

The quickest way to verify OSPF convergence is to use the _____ command to view the routing table for each router in the topology.

 Lab - Configuring Basic Single-Area OSPFv2 (SN 5.1.1.9)

Identify Network Types

Match the definition on the left with the network type on the right. This is a one-to-one matching exercise.

Definitions

_____ Connects distant OSPF networks to the backbone area

_____ Connects multiple routers using Frame Relay

_____ Connects multiple routers in a hub-and-spoke topology

_____ Connects two routers directly on a single WAN network

_____ Connects multiple routers using Ethernet technology

Network Type

a. Broadcast multi-access

b. Nonbroadcast multi-access

c. Point to multipoint

d. Point to point

e. Virtual links

In Figure 5-3, label each network type.

Figure 5-3   Network Types

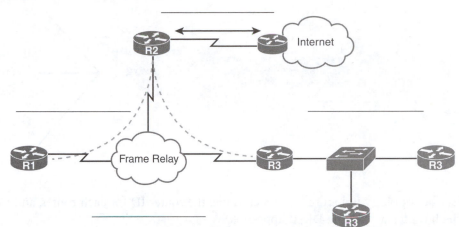

OSPF and Multi-Access Networks

A multi-access network is a network with more than two devices on the same shared media. Examples of multi-access networks include Ethernet and Frame Relay. Frame Relay is a WAN technology that is discussed in a later CCNA course. The following exercises cover the concepts of multi-access networks in OSPF and the DR/BDR election process.

OSPF and Multi-Access Networks Completion Exercise

Complete the missing words or phrases in the following paragraphs.

On multi-access networks (networks supporting more than two routers) such as Ethernet and Frame-Relay networks, the hello protocol elects a _____ (DR) and a _____ (BDR). Among other things, the _____ is responsible for generating LSAs for the entire multi-access network which allows a reduction in routing update traffic.

The DR, BDR, and every other router in an OSPF network sends out Hellos using _____ as the destination address. If a DRother (a router that is not the DR) needs to send a link-state advertisement (LSA), it will send it using _____ as the destination address. The DR and the BDR will receive LSAs at this address.

The DR/BDR election is based on OSPF _____ and OSPF router _____ . By default, all OSPF routers have a _____ of _____ . If all OSPF routers have the same _____ , the highest router _____ determines the DR and BDR.

If the router _____ is not explicitly configured and a loopback interface is not configured, the _____ IP address on an active interface at the moment of OSPF process startup is used as the router _____ .

In Figure 5-4, label the steps taken to elect the DR.

Figure 5-4   Steps in the DR Election Process

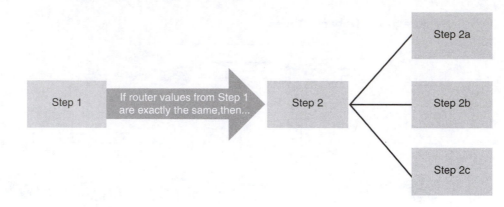

Use the topology in Figure 5-5 to determine the router ID for each router, and then determine which router will be the DR, if applicable.

Figure 5-5   Determine the Router ID

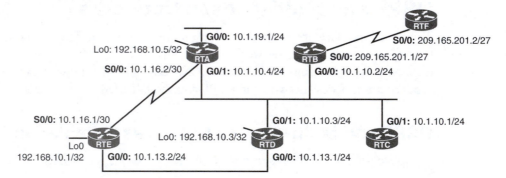

In Table 5-3, record the router ID for each router.

Table 5-3   Listing of Router IDs

Device	Router ID
Router A	
Router B	
Router C	
Router D	
Router E	
Router F	

In Table 5-4, determine whether a DR will be elected for each network and record the DR's hostname. If no DR is elected, indicate so with "none."

Table 5-4   **Listing of DRs**

Network	DR
209.165.201.0	
10.1.16.0	
10.1.13.0	
10.1.10.0	

Note: Configure your OSPFv2 routers with a router ID to control the DR/BDR election. With OSPFv3, you must configure a router ID.

Setting the priority on the interface is another way to control DR or BDR.

In addition to configuring loopbacks, it is a good idea to configure RTA with an OSPF priority that will ensure it always wins the DR/BDR election. The syntax for configuring OSPF priority is as follows:

Document the commands you use to configure on RTA to make sure that its priority will always win the DR/BDR election.

DR/BDR Election Exercise

In the following exercises, assume that all routers are simultaneously booted and that router priorities are set to the default. Determine the network type, if applicable, and label which router is elected as the DR and which router is elected as the BDR.

Refer to Figure 5-6 and answer the following questions.

Figure 5-6   DR/BDR Election Exercise 1 Topology

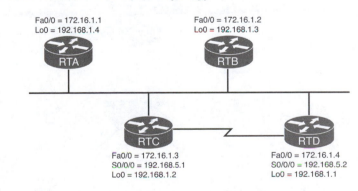

What is the router ID for RTA?

What is the router ID for RTB?

What is the router ID for RTC?

What is the router ID for RTD?

Which router will be elected DR?

Which router will be elected BDR?

Refer to Figure 5-7 and determine whether there will be a DR/BDR election. If applicable, designate which router is DR and which router is BDR.

Figure 5-7   DR/BDR Election Exercise 2 Topology

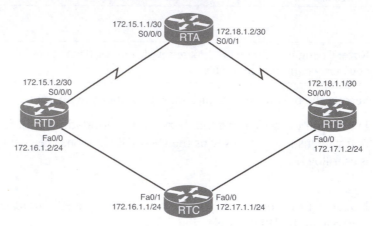

Network	DR/BDR Election?	Which Router Is the DR?	Which Router Is the BDR?
172.15.1.0/30			
172.16.1.0/24			
172.17.1.0/24			
172.18.1.0/30			

Refer to Figure 5-8 and answer the following questions.

Figure 5-8   DR/BDR Election Exercise 3 Topology

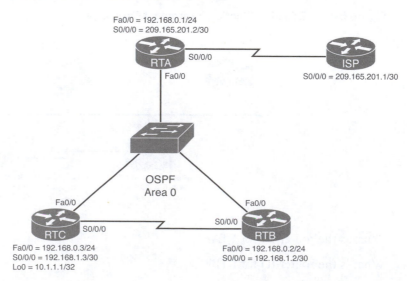

What is the router ID for RTA?

What is the router ID for RTB?

What is the router ID for RTC?

Which router is DR for the 192.168.0.0/24 network?

Which router is BDR for the 192.168.0.0/24 network?

Now assume a priority of zero on RTA. Which router is DR for the 192.168.1.0/24 network?

What will happen if another router, RTD, joins the 192.168.0.0/24 network with a router ID of 209.165.201.9?

Redistributing an OSPF Default Route Exercise

In some topology configurations and routing policy situations, it is desirable to have an Autonomous System Boundary Router (ASBR) redistribute a default route to the OSPF neighbors in the area. This can be quickly accomplished in both OSPFv2 and OSPFv3.

OSPFv2 Default Route Redistribution

In Figure 5-9, notice that RTA is now our gateway router because it provides access outside the area. In OSPF terminology, RTA is called the _____ (ASBR) because it connects to an external routing domain that uses a different routing policy.

Figure 5-9   Propagating a Default Route in OSPFv2

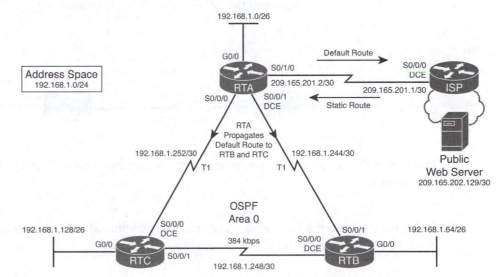

Each routing protocol handles the propagation of default routing information a little differently. For OSPF, the gateway router must be configured with two commands. First, RTA will need a static default route pointing to ISP. Document the command to configure a static default route on RTA using the *exit interface* argument.

Using the *exit interface* argument, document the command necessary to configure ISP with a static route pointing to the 192.168.1.0/24 address space.

At this point, any host on the LAN attached to RTA will be able to access ISP and be able to ping the Public Web Server at 209.165.202.129. However, RTB and RTC still cannot ping outside the 192.168.1.0/24 address space. Why?

Document the command that needs to be configured on RTA to fix this problem.

OSPFv3 Default Route Redistribution

Configuring OSPFv3 to propagate a default route is essentially the same tasks as you do in OSPFv2. Figure 5-10 is an IPv6 version of Figure 5-9.

Figure 5-10   Propagating a Default Route in OSPFv3

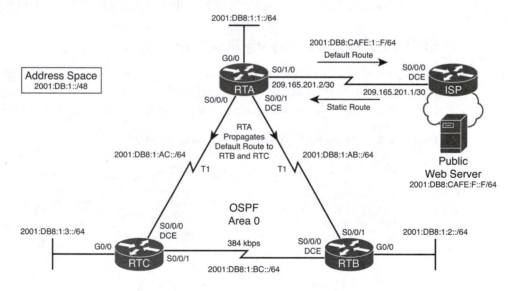

Document the command to configure a static default route on RTA using the *exit interface* argument.

Using the *exit interface* argument, document the command necessary to configure ISP with a static route pointing to the 2001:DB8:1::/48 address space.

Document the command that will cause RTA to propagate the default router to RTB and RTC.

```
RTA(config-rtr)#default-information originate
```

Fine-Tuning OSPF Interfaces

OSPF routers must use matching Hello intervals and Dead intervals on the same link. The default interval values result in efficient OSPF operation and seldom need to be modified. However, you can change them.

Again, refer to Figure 5-9. Assuming that the current intervals are 10 and 40, document the commands necessary to change these OSPFv2 intervals on the link between RTB and RTC to a value four times greater than the current value.

Note that it is not necessary to configure the Dead interval as long as the desired interval is four times the Hello. The IOS will automatically increase the Dead interval to four times the configured Hello interval.

Now refer to Figure 5-10. Assuming that the current intervals are 10 and 40, document the commands necessary to change the OSPFv3 intervals on the link between RTB and RTC to a value four times greater than the current value.

Other than the **show run** command, what commands can you use to verify OSPF timers on an interface for both IPv4 and IPv6?

Securing OSPFv2 with MD5 Authentication

Because routers are targets for network attacks, you should always configure authentication services for OSPFv2 using the strongest authentication available: MD5 (message digest algorithm 5).

Assume the routers in Figure 5-11 are using MD5 authentication to exchange OSPFv2 routing updates. Briefly explain the steps in MD5 authentication as R1 sends an OSPF message to R2.

Figure 5-11   OSPFv2 MD5 Authentication Between R1 and R2

You can configure OSPFv2 MD5 authentication globally, forcing all OSPF interfaces to use authentication. Or you can configure authentication on specific interfaces.

Document the command syntax, including the router prompt, to enable OSPFv2 MD5 authentication on all interfaces.

Document the command syntax including the router prompt to enable OSPFv2 MD5 authentication only on specific interfaces.

Refer to Figure 5-9. Document the commands to configure RTA to use MD5 authentication globally on all OSPF interfaces. Choose your own process ID and key values.

```
RTA(config-if)# ip ospf message-digest-key 1 md5 cisco123
RTA(config-if)# interface s0/0/1
RTA(config-if)# ip ospf message-digest-key 1 md5 cisco123
```

Document the commands to configure RTB to use MD5 authentication on the serial interfaces only. Choose your own process ID and key values.

What command can you use to verify OSPF MD5 authentication?

Note: Cisco IOS supports a simple authentication method. However, this method sends the password in plain text. Therefore, it is not considered a best practice.

Lab - Configuring OSPFv2 Advance Features (SN 5.1.5.8/RP 7.1.4.8)

Packet Tracer - Configuring OSPFv2 Advance Features (SN 5.1.5.7/RP 7.1.4.7)

Troubleshooting Single-Area OSPF Implementations

Troubleshooting single-area OSPF is required skill for any network professional involved in the implementation and maintenance of an OSPF network. Solid understanding of OSPF operation and the impact of the OSPF configuration commands is essential.

OSPF Adjacency Issues

A common problem in OSPF convergence is a lack of adjacency with OSPF neighbors. List at least four reasons why adjacency might fail to establish.

-
-
-
-
-
-

What are the OSPFv2 and OSPFv3 commands you use to quickly verify adjacency between OSPF routers?

The command will list a state for each known OSPF router. What are the seven states OSPF transitions through on its way to convergence?

Identify OSPFv2 Troubleshooting Commands

The following output is from the topology shown in Figure 5-9. Indicate the command used to generate the output.

```
RTA# _____

Codes: L - local, C - connected, S - static, R - RIP, M - mobile, B - BGP
       D - EIGRP, EX - EIGRP external, O - OSPF, IA - OSPF inter area
       N1 - OSPF NSSA external type 1, N2 - OSPF NSSA external type 2
       E1 - OSPF external type 1, E2 - OSPF external type 2
       i - IS-IS, su - IS-IS summary, L1 - IS-IS level-1, L2 - IS-IS level-2
       ia - IS-IS inter area, * - candidate default, U - per-user static route
```

```
              o - ODR, P - periodic downloaded static route, H - NHRP, l - LISP
              + - replicated route, % - next hop override

Gateway of last resort is 0.0.0.0 to network 0.0.0.0


      192.168.1.0/24 is variably subnetted, 9 subnets, 3 masks
O        192.168.1.64/26 [110/65] via 192.168.1.246, 00:19:35, Serial0/0/1
O        192.168.1.128/26 [110/65] via 192.168.1.254, 00:19:10, Serial0/0/0
O        192.168.1.248/30 [110/128] via 192.168.1.254, 00:19:10, Serial0/0/0
                          [110/128] via 192.168.1.246, 00:19:35, Serial0/0/1
```

RTA# _____

```
Neighbor ID      Pri   State        Dead Time   Address        Interface
192.168.1.254     0    FULL/  -     00:00:31    192.168.1.254   Serial0/0/0
192.168.1.249     0    FULL/  -     00:00:32    192.168.1.246   Serial0/0/1
```

RTA# _____

```
Serial0/0/0 is up, line protocol is up
  Internet Address 192.168.1.253/30, Area 0, Attached via Network Statement
  Process ID 1, Router ID 192.168.1.253, Network Type POINT_TO_POINT, Cost: 64
  Topology-MTID    Cost    Disabled    Shutdown      Topology Name
       0           64        no          no            Base
  Transmit Delay is 1 sec, State POINT_TO_POINT
  Timer intervals configured, Hello 10, Dead 40, Wait 40, Retransmit 5
    oob-resync timeout 40
    Hello due in 00:00:03
  Supports Link-local Signaling (LLS)
  Cisco NSF helper support enabled
  IETF NSF helper support enabled
  Index 3/3, flood queue length 0
  Next 0x0(0)/0x0(0)
  Last flood scan length is 1, maximum is 1
  Last flood scan time is 0 msec, maximum is 0 msec
  Neighbor Count is 1, Adjacent neighbor count is 1
    Adjacent with neighbor 192.168.1.254
  Suppress hello for 0 neighbor(s)
```

RTA# _____

```
*** IP Routing is NSF aware ***

Routing Protocol is "ospf 1"
  Outgoing update filter list for all interfaces is not set
  Incoming update filter list for all interfaces is not set
  Router ID 192.168.1.253
  It is an autonomous system boundary router
```

```
Redistributing External Routes from,
 Number of areas in this router is 1. 1 normal 0 stub 0 nssa
 Maximum path: 4
 Routing for Networks:
    192.168.1.0 0.0.0.63 area 0
    192.168.1.244 0.0.0.3 area 0
    192.168.1.252 0.0.0.3 area 0
 Routing Information Sources:
    Gateway         Distance      Last Update
    192.168.1.246        110       00:18:13
    192.168.1.254        110       00:17:48
 Distance: (default is 110)
```

```
RTA# _____
Routing Process "ospf 1" with ID 192.168.1.253
Start time: 00:44:46.536, Time elapsed: 00:23:27.360
Supports only single TOS(TOS0) routes
Supports opaque LSA
Supports Link-local Signaling (LLS)
Supports area transit capability
Supports NSSA (compatible with RFC 3101)
Event-log enabled, Maximum number of events: 1000, Mode: cyclic
It is an autonomous system boundary router
Redistributing External Routes from,
Router is not originating router-LSAs with maximum metric
Initial SPF schedule delay 5000 msecs
Minimum hold time between two consecutive SPFs 10000 msecs
Maximum wait time between two consecutive SPFs 10000 msecs
Incremental-SPF disabled
Minimum LSA interval 5 secs
Minimum LSA arrival 1000 msecs
LSA group pacing timer 240 secs
Interface flood pacing timer 33 msecs
Retransmission pacing timer 66 msecs
Number of external LSA 1. Checksum Sum 0x003416
Number of opaque AS LSA 0. Checksum Sum 0x000000
Number of DCbitless external and opaque AS LSA 0
Number of DoNotAge external and opaque AS LSA 0
Number of areas in this router is 1. 1 normal 0 stub 0 nssa
Number of areas transit capable is 0
External flood list length 0
IETF NSF helper support enabled
Cisco NSF helper support enabled
```

```
Reference bandwidth unit is 100 mbps
    Area BACKBONE(0)
        Number of interfaces in this area is 3
        Area has no authentication
        SPF algorithm last executed 00:16:47.472 ago
        SPF algorithm executed 4 times
        Area ranges are
        Number of LSA 3. Checksum Sum 0x00E037
        Number of opaque link LSA 0. Checksum Sum 0x000000
        Number of DCbitless LSA 0
        Number of indication LSA 0
        Number of DoNotAge LSA 0
        Flood list length 0
```

Identify OSPFv3 Troubleshooting Commands

The following output is from the topology shown in Figure 5-10. Indicate the command used to generate the output.

```
RTC# _____

IPv6 Routing Protocol is "connected"

IPv6 Routing Protocol is "ND"

IPv6 Routing Protocol is "ospf 1"

  Router ID 3.3.3.3

  Number of areas: 1 normal, 0 stub, 0 nssa

  Interfaces (Area 0):

    GigabitEthernet0/0

    Serial0/0/1

    Serial0/0/0

  Redistribution:

    None
```

```
RTC# _____


            OSPFv3 Router with ID (3.3.3.3) (Process ID 1)
```

Neighbor ID	Pri	State		Dead Time	Interface ID	Interface
2.2.2.2	0	FULL/	-	00:00:39	6	Serial0/0/1
1.1.1.1	0	FULL/	-	00:00:31	6	Serial0/0/0

```
RTC# _____

Serial0/0/1 is up, line protocol is up

  Link Local Address FE80::C, Interface ID 7

  Area 0, Process ID 1, Instance ID 0, Router ID 3.3.3.3

  Network Type POINT_TO_POINT, Cost: 64

  Transmit Delay is 1 sec, State POINT_TO_POINT
```

```
    Timer intervals configured, Hello 10, Dead 40, Wait 40, Retransmit 5
      Hello due in 00:00:06
    Graceful restart helper support enabled
    Index 1/2/2, flood queue length 0
    Next 0x0(0)/0x0(0)/0x0(0)
    Last flood scan length is 2, maximum is 4
    Last flood scan time is 0 msec, maximum is 0 msec
    Neighbor Count is 1, Adjacent neighbor count is 1
      Adjacent with neighbor 2.2.2.2
    Suppress hello for 0 neighbor(s)
```

```
RTC# _____
Routing Process "ospfv3 1" with ID 3.3.3.3
Event-log enabled, Maximum number of events: 1000, Mode: cyclic
Router is not originating router-LSAs with maximum metric
Initial SPF schedule delay 5000 msecs
Minimum hold time between two consecutive SPFs 10000 msecs
Maximum wait time between two consecutive SPFs 10000 msecs
Minimum LSA interval 5 secs
Minimum LSA arrival 1000 msecs
LSA group pacing timer 240 secs
Interface flood pacing timer 33 msecs
Retransmission pacing timer 66 msecs
Number of external LSA 1. Checksum Sum 0x00B657
Number of areas in this router is 1. 1 normal 0 stub 0 nssa
Graceful restart helper support enabled
Reference bandwidth unit is 100 mbps
RFC1583 compatibility enabled
    Area BACKBONE(0)
        Number of interfaces in this area is 3
        SPF algorithm executed 4 times
        Number of LSA 15. Checksum Sum 0x07E293
        Number of DCbitless LSA 0
        Number of indication LSA 0
        Number of DoNotAge LSA 0
        Flood list length 0
```

```
RTC#_____
IPv6 Routing Table - default - 11 entries
Codes: C - Connected, L - Local, S - Static, U - Per-user Static route
       B - BGP, R - RIP, I1 - ISIS L1, I2 - ISIS L2
       IA - ISIS interarea, IS - ISIS summary, D - EIGRP, EX - EIGRP external
       ND - ND Default, NDp - ND Prefix, DCE - Destination, NDr - Redirect
       O - OSPF Intra, OI - OSPF Inter, OE1 - OSPF ext 1, OE2 - OSPF ext 2
       ON1 - OSPF NSSA ext 1, ON2 - OSPF NSSA ext 2
```

```
OE2 ::/0 [110/1], tag 1
     via FE80::A, GigabitEthernet0/0
O    2001:DB8:1:1::/64 [110/1]
     via GigabitEthernet0/0, directly connected
O    2001:DB8:1:AB::/64 [110/65]
     via FE80::B, GigabitEthernet0/0
O    2001:DB8:2:1::/64 [110/1]
     via GigabitEthernet0/0, directly connected
```

Lab - Troubleshooting Basic Single-Area OSPFv2 and OSPFv3 (SN 5.2.3.3/RP 7.2.3.3)

Lab - Troubleshooting Advanced Single-Area OSPFv2 (SN 5.2.3.4/RP 7.2.3.4)

Packet Tracer - Troubleshooting Single-Area OSPFv2 (SN 5.2.2.3/RP 7.2.2.3)

Packet Tracer - Skills Integration Challenge (SN 5.3.1.2/RP 7.3.1.2)

CHAPTER 6

Multiarea OSPF

In larger network implementations, single-area OSPF can require a significant amount of CPU and memory resources. As the number of routers grows, network administrators often implement multiarea OSPF to control the size of link-state databases, routing table entries, and the number of SPF calculations. This chapter reviews the concepts and configurations for multiarea OSPFv2 and OSPFv3.

Multiarea OSPF Operation

Multiarea OSPF was specifically designed to address several issues that result from single-area OSPF growing beyond its constraints.

Multiarea OSPF Terminology and Concepts

Briefly describe three issues that arise if an OSPF area becomes too big.

-

-

-

Briefly describe the role of each of the following OSPF router types.

- Internal router:

- Backbone router:

- Area Border Router (ABR):

- Autonomous System Boundary Router (ASBR):

In Table 6-1, indicate the OSPF router type for each router in Figure 6-1. A router can be more than one type.

Figure 6-1   Sample Multiarea OSPF Topology

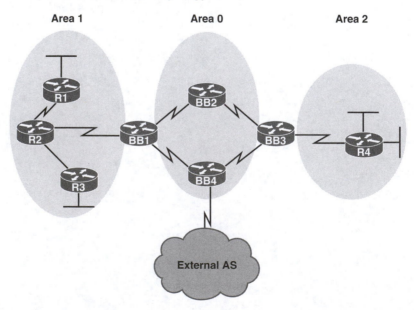

Table 6-1   Indentify the OSPF Router Type

OSPF Router Type	BB1	BB2	BB3	BB4	R1	R2	R3	R4
Internal router								
Backbone router								
Area Border Router (ABR)								
Autonomous System Boundary Router (ASBR)								

Multiarea OSPF LSA Operation

Although the RFCs for OSPF specify up to 11 different LSA types, at the CCNA level we are only concerned with the first 5. In Table 6-2, indicate the name for each LSA type.

Table 6-2   Most Common OSPF LSA Types

LSA Type	Description
1	
2	
3 and 4	
5	

Refer to Figure 6-1. In Table 6-3, indicate which LSA type is used in each of the scenarios.

Table 6-3   Determine the LSA Type

LSA Scenario	Type 1	Type 2	Type 3	Type 4	Type 5
BB1 is advertising to Area 1 a link to an external autonomous system.					
BB1 and BB3 do not forward these LSAs into Area 0.					
As DR, R2 sends this LSA type to R3.					
BB4 is advertising an external network to BB3 and BB1.					
BB3 is advertising to Area 2 that BB4 is the ASBR.					
BB2 is advertising its directly connected OSPF-enabled links to BB1 and BB3.					
BB2 is advertising the links in Area 0 to the routers in Area 1.					

OSPF Routing Table and Types of Routes

Because of the different LSA types with routes originating from different areas and from non-OSPF networks, the routing table uses different codes to identify the various types of routes.

Refer to Example 6-1. Briefly describe each of the three OSPF route types shown.

Example 6-1   A Sample Multiarea OSPF Routing Table

```
BB1# show ip route | begin Gateway
Gateway of last resort is 10.0.0.1 to network 0.0.0.0


O*E2  0.0.0.0/0 [110/1] via 10.0.0.1, 00:02:16, Serial0/0/0
      10.0.0.0/8 is variably subnetted, 3 subnets, 2 masks
C        10.0.0.0/30 is directly connected, Serial0/0/0
L        10.0.0.2/32 is directly connected, Serial0/0/0
O        10.0.1.0/30 [110/128] via 10.0.0.1, 00:03:24, Serial0/0/0
      172.16.0.0/16 is variably subnetted, 7 subnets, 4 masks
C        172.16.0.0/23 is directly connected, GigabitEthernet0/0
L        172.16.0.1/32 is directly connected, GigabitEthernet0/0
C        172.16.2.0/23 is directly connected, GigabitEthernet0/1
L        172.16.2.1/32 is directly connected, GigabitEthernet0/1
O        172.16.5.0/24 [110/65] via 10.0.0.1, 00:03:24, Serial0/0/0
O IA     172.16.16.0/21 [110/129] via 10.0.0.1, 00:03:24, Serial0/0/0
O IA     172.16.24.0/21 [110/129] via 10.0.0.1, 00:03:24, Serial0/0/0
BB1#
```

List the steps in order that OSPF uses to calculate the best paths.

Configuring Multiarea OSPF

At the CCNA level, the configuration of multiarea OSPF is rather straightforward if you are already comfortable configuring single-area OSPF. This section reviews configuring and verifying multiarea OSPFv2 and OSPFv3.

Configuring Multiarea OSPF

We will use the topology in Figure 6-2 and the addressing in Table 6-4 to configure a dual-stack network running multiarea OSPFv2 and OSPFv3.

Figure 6-2 Dual-Stacked Multiarea OSPF Topology

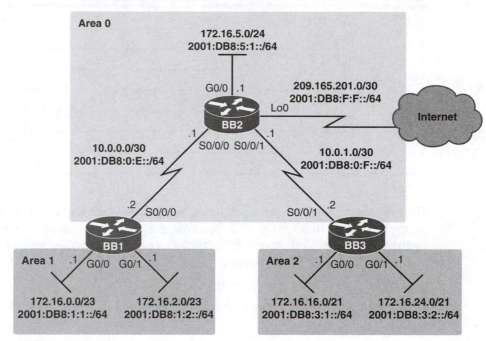

Based on the addressing shown in the topology, finish documenting the addressing scheme in Table 6-4.

Table 6-4 Addressing for the Dual-Stacked Multiarea OSPF Topology

Device	Interface	Addressing Information	
BB1	G0/0	172.16.0.0	255.255.254.0
		2001:DB8:1:1::2/64	
	G0/1	172.16.2.0	255.255.254.0
		2001:DB8:1:2::2/64	
	S0/0/0	10.0.0.2	255.255.255.252
		2001:DB8:0:E::2/64	
	Link-Local	FE80::1	
	Router ID	1.1.1.1	
BB2	G0/0		
	S0/0/0		
	S0/0/1		
	Lo0		
	Link-Local		
	Router ID		

Device	Interface	Addressing Information
BB3	G0/0	
	G0/1	
	S0/0/1	
	Link-Local	
	Router ID	

The only difference between configuring single-area OSPF and multiarea OSPF is assigning the area value. Recall that for OSPFv2, you configure the area as part of the **network** command in OSPF router configuration mode. In OSPFv3, you configure the area as part of the **ipv6 ospf** command in interface configuration mode.

Document the OSPFv2 and OSPFv3 routing configurations for all three routers. Include default routing to the Internet with BB2 redistributing the IPv4 and IPv6 default routes to BB1 and BB2.

_____

_____

_____

_____

_____

_____

_____

_____

_____

_____

_____

_____

_____

_____

_____

_____

_____

_____

_____

_____

_____

Configuring Route Summarization for Multiarea OSPFv2

ABRs do not automatically summarize network addresses across area boundaries. To reduce the size of routing tables, you can manually configure ABRs and ASBRs to summarize networks so that they will then inject them into another area. In Figure 6-2, BB1 and BB3 can summarize the two LANs into one network advertisement.

What is the command syntax to configure an ABR interarea summary route?

```
Router(config-router)# area area-id range address mask
```

What is the summary route for the two LANs attached to BB1:

Address: _____   Mask: _____

Document the command to configure BB1 with an interarea summary route.

```
BB1(config-router)# area 1 range 172.16.0.0 255.255.252.0
```

What is the summary route for the two LANs attached to BB3:

Address: _____   Mask: _____

Document the command to configure BB3 with an interarea summary route.

```
BB3(config-router)# area 2 range 172.16.16.0 255.255.240.0
```

Your OSPF routing tables should look like the output in Example 6-2.

Example 6-2   Multiarea OSPFv2 and OSPFv3 Routing Tables

```
BB1# show ip route ospf | begin Gateway

Gateway of last resort is 10.0.0.1 to network 0.0.0.0


O*E2  0.0.0.0/0 [110/1] via 10.0.0.1, 00:08:36, Serial0/0/0
      10.0.0.0/8 is variably subnetted, 3 subnets, 2 masks
O        10.0.1.0/30 [110/128] via 10.0.0.1, 00:08:36, Serial0/0/0
      172.16.0.0/16 is variably subnetted, 7 subnets, 5 masks
O        172.16.0.0/22 is a summary, 00:08:36, Null0
O        172.16.5.0/24 [110/65] via 10.0.0.1, 00:08:36, Serial0/0/0
O IA     172.16.16.0/20 [110/129] via 10.0.0.1, 00:04:44, Serial0/0/0
BB1# show ipv6 route ospf | begin OE2
        OE2 - OSPF ext 2, ON1 - OSPF NSSA ext 1, ON2 - OSPF NSSA ext 2
OE2 ::/0 [110/1], tag 10
     via FE80::2, Serial0/0/0
O   2001:DB8:0:F::/64 [110/128]
     via FE80::2, Serial0/0/0
OI  2001:DB8:3:1::/64 [110/129]
     via FE80::2, Serial0/0/0
OI  2001:DB8:3:2::/64 [110/129]
     via FE80::2, Serial0/0/0
O   2001:DB8:5:1::/64 [110/65]
     via FE80::2, Serial0/0/0
BB1#
```

```
BB2# show ip route ospf | begin Gateway

Gateway of last resort is 0.0.0.0 to network 0.0.0.0


     172.16.0.0/16 is variably subnetted, 4 subnets, 4 masks
O IA     172.16.0.0/22 [110/65] via 10.0.0.2, 00:09:51, Serial0/0/0
O IA     172.16.16.0/20 [110/65] via 10.0.1.2, 00:05:59, Serial0/0/1
BB2# show ipv6 route ospf | begin OI  2001
OI  2001:DB8:1:1::/64 [110/65]
     via FE80::1, Serial0/0/0
OI  2001:DB8:1:2::/64 [110/65]
     via FE80::1, Serial0/0/0
OI  2001:DB8:3:1::/64 [110/65]
     via FE80::3, Serial0/0/1
OI  2001:DB8:3:2::/64 [110/65]
     via FE80::3, Serial0/0/1
BB2#
```

```
BB3# show ip route ospf | begin Gateway

Gateway of last resort is 10.0.1.1 to network 0.0.0.0
```

```
O*E2   0.0.0.0/0 [110/1] via 10.0.1.1, 00:05:31, Serial0/0/1
        10.0.0.0/8 is variably subnetted, 3 subnets, 2 masks
O          10.0.0.0/30 [110/128] via 10.0.1.1, 00:05:31, Serial0/0/1
        172.16.0.0/16 is variably subnetted, 7 subnets, 5 masks
O IA     172.16.0.0/22 [110/129] via 10.0.1.1, 00:05:31, Serial0/0/1
O        172.16.5.0/24 [110/65] via 10.0.1.1, 00:05:31, Serial0/0/1
O        172.16.16.0/20 is a summary, 00:05:31, Null0
BB3# show ipv6 route ospf | begin OE2
        OE2 - OSPF ext 2, ON1 - OSPF NSSA ext 1, ON2 - OSPF NSSA ext 2
OE2 ::/0 [110/1], tag 10
     via FE80::2, Serial0/0/1
O    2001:DB8:0:E::/64 [110/128]
     via FE80::2, Serial0/0/1
OI   2001:DB8:1:1::/64 [110/129]
     via FE80::2, Serial0/0/1
OI   2001:DB8:1:2::/64 [110/129]
     via FE80::2, Serial0/0/1
O    2001:DB8:5:1::/64 [110/65]
     via FE80::2, Serial0/0/1
BB3#
```

Verifying Multiarea OSPF

In Table 6-5, indicate which command or commands will provide the multiarea OSPFv2 verification information.

Table 6-5   Multiarea OSPFv2 Verification Commands

Verification Information	show ip protocols	show ip ospf interface brief	show ip route ospf	show ip ospf database
Process ID				
State of OSPF Interface				
Networks Configured				
Interface Cost				
Router ID				
Administrative Distance				
Number of Areas				
Networks from Other Areas				
All Known Routes				
Total Cost of Route				

Verification commands for multiarea OSPFv3 are almost identical to OSPFv2. In Table 6-6, indicate which command or commands will provide the multiarea OSPFv3 verification information.

Table 6-6   Multiarea OSPFv3 Verification Commands

Verification Information	show ipv6 protocols	show ipv6 ospf interface brief	show ipv6 route ospf	show ipv6 ospf database
Administrative Distance				
All Known Routes				
Interface Cost				
Networks from Other Areas				
Number of Areas				
Process ID				
Router ID				
State of OSPF Interface				
Total Cost of Route				

Lab - Configuring Multiarea OSPFv2 (SN 6.2.3.8/RP 8.2.3.8)

Lab - Configuring Multiarea OSPFv3 (SN 6.2.3.9/RP 8.2.3.9)

Lab - Troubleshooting Multiarea OSPFv2 and OSPFv3 (SN 6.2.3.10/RP 8.2.3.10)

Packet Tracer
☐ Activity

Packet Tracer - Configuring Multiarea OSPFv2 (SN 6.2.3.6/RP 8.2.3.6)

Packet Tracer - Configuring Multiarea OSPFv3 (SN 6.2.3.7/RP 8.2.3.7)

CHAPTER 7

EIGRP

The main purpose in Cisco's development of Enhanced Interior Gateway Routing Protocol (EIGRP) was to create a classless version of IGRP. EIGRP includes several features that are not commonly found in other distance vector routing protocols such as RIP (RIPv1 and RIPv2) and IGRP. Although EIGRP may act like a link-state routing protocol, it is still a distance vector routing protocol.

Characteristics of EIGRP

EIGRP is considered an advanced distance vector routing protocol because it has characteristics not found in other distance vector protocols like RIP and IGRP.

Describe Basic EIGRP Features

A major difference between EIGRP and other distance vector protocols is the algorithm it uses to calculate the best rate. Name and briefly describe this algorithm.

What protocol, unique to EIGRP, provides for the delivery of EIGRP packets to neighbors?

What is meant by the statement, "EIGRP provides partial and bounded updates"?

Protocol-dependent modules (PDMs) allow EIGRP to route several different network layer protocols. List at least four functions of EIGRP's PDMs.

-
-
-
-
-
-

What are the IPv4 and IPv6 multicast addresses used by EIGRP's RTP?

Identify and Describe EIGRP Packet Types

Like the Open Shortest Path First (OSPF) Protocol, EIGRP relies on different types of packets to maintain its tables and establish relationships with neighbor routers. In Table 7-1, provide a brief description for each EIGRP packet type.

Table 7-1   EIGRP Packet Types

Packet Type	Description
Hello	
Acknowledgment	
Update	
Query	
Reply	

Complete the missing elements in this exercise by filling in appropriate words or phrases. When encountered, circle whether the packet is reliable or unreliable and whether it is unicast or multicast.

Hello packets:

- (Reliable/unreliable) (unicast/multicast) sent to the address, _____, to discover and maintain neighbors; contains the router's neighbor table

- Default _____ interval depends on the bandwidth:

    - ≤ 1.544 Mbps = __ sec. _____ interval (_____ holdtime)

    - > 1.544 Mbps = _ sec. _____ interval (_____ holdtime)

Update packets. Sent (reliably/unreliably), there are two types:

- (Unicast/multicast) to new neighbor discovered; contains routing information

- (Unicast/multicast) to all neighbors when topology changes

Query packets. Queries are (unicast/multicast) (reliably/unreliably) during route recomputation, asking neighbors for a new successor to a lost route.

Reply packets. Neighbors (unicast/multicast) a reply to a query whether they have a route.

Acknowledgment packets. "Dataless" (unicast/multicast) packet that acknowledges the receipt of a packet that was sent reliably. This type is actually a Hello packet with a nonzero value in the Acknowledgment field.

An EIGRP router assumes that as long as it is receiving Hello packets from a neighbor, the neighbor and its routes remain viable. _____ tells the router the maximum time the router should wait to receive the next Hello before declaring that neighbor as _____. By default, this waiting period is _____ times the _____ interval, or _____ seconds on most networks and _____ seconds on networks with speeds of T1 or slower. If the time expires, EIGRP will declare the route as down, and DUAL will search for a new path by sending out queries.

Identify Elements of the EIGRP Message Formats

Figure 7-1 shows an example of an encapsulated EIGRP message. Fill in the missing field contents.

Figure 7-1   Encapsulated EIGRP Message

Data Link Frame Header	IP Packet Header	EIGRP Packet Header	Type/Length/Values Types

Data Link Frame

MAC Source Address = Address of Sending Interface
MAC Destination Address = Multicast: 01-00-5E-00-00-0A

> IP Packet
>
> IP Source Address = Address of Sending Interface
> IP Destination Address = Multicast: [   ]
> Protocol Field = [ ] for EIGRP

> > EIGRP Packet Header
> >
> > Opcode for EIGRP Packet Type
> > [   ]

> > > TLV Types
> > >
> > > Some Types Include:
> > > 0x0001 [   ]
> > > 0x0102 [   ]
> > > 0x0103 [   ]

The EIGRP packet _____ is included with every EIGRP packet, regardless of its type. In the IP packet header, the Protocol field is set to _____ to indicate EIGRP, and the destination address is set to the multicast _____.

Every EIGRP message includes the header as shown in Figure 7-2. Fill in the missing field contents.

Figure 7-2   EIGRP Packet Header

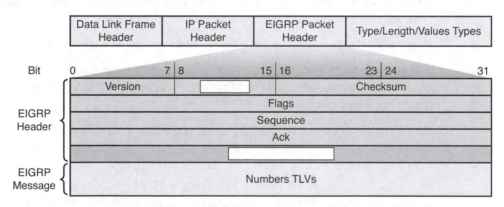

Important fields for our discussion include the _____ field and the _____ (AS) field. _____ specifies the EIGRP packet type, one of the following:

- ▪
- ▪
- ▪
- ▪

The number in the AS field is used to track multiple instances of EIGRP.

Encapsulated in the EIGRP packet header is the TLV (Type/Length/Values) shown in Figure 7-3. Fill in the missing field contents.

Figure 7-3   EIGRP Parameters TLV

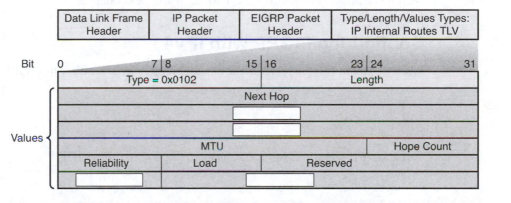

This EIGRP parameters message includes the weights that EIGRP uses for its _____ metric. By default, only _____ and _____ are weighted. Both are equally weighted; therefore, the _____ field for _____ and the _____ field for _____ are both set to _____ . The other K values are set to _____.

The _____ is the amount of time the EIGRP neighbor receiving this message should wait before considering the advertising router to be down.

Figure 7-4 shows the IP Internal message that is used to advertise EIGRP routes within an autonomous system. Fill in the missing field contents.

Figure 7-4   IP Internal Routes TLV

Important fields include the metric fields (_____ and _____), the subnet mask field (_____), and the _____ field.

Explain how the delay value is calculated?

Explain how the bandwidth value is determined?

The subnet mask is specified as the _____ or the number of _____ bits in the subnet mask. For example, the subnet mask 255.255.255.0 has a _____ of _____.

Figure 7-5 shows the IP External message that is used when external routes are imported into the EIGRP routing process. Notice that the bottom half of the IP External TLV includes all the fields used by the IP Internal TLV. Fill in the missing field contents.

Figure 7-5   IP External Routes TLV

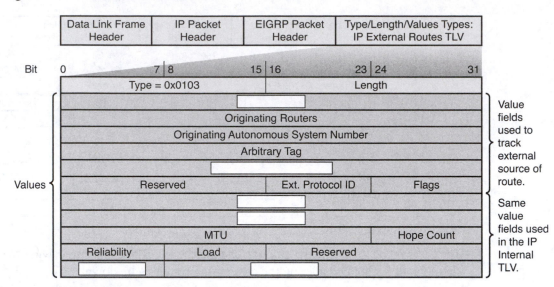

Configuring EIGRP for IPv4

Implementing EIGRP for IPv4 is with basic configurations is straightforward. Tweaking EIGRP with more advanced settings is the topic of the next chapter.

Configuring EIGRP with IPv4

Briefly explain the purpose of the autonomous system number in EIGRP configurations.

What are the steps a Cisco router uses to choose its router ID?

What are the two main reasons for using the **passive-interface** command?

We will use the topology in Figure 7-6 and the addressing in Table 7-2 to configure a dual-stack network running EIGRP for IPv4 and IPv6.

Figure 7-6 **Dual-Stacked Multiarea EIGRP Topology**

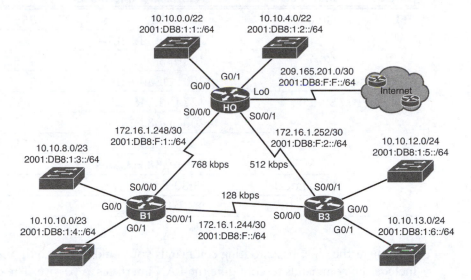

Table 7-2 **Addressing for the Dual-Stacked EIGRP Topology**

Device	Interface	Addressing Information	
HQ	G0/0	10.10.0.1	255.255.252.0
		2001:DB8:1:1::1/64	
	G0/1	10.10.4.1	255.255.252.0
		2001:DB8:1:2::1/64	
	S0/0/0	172.16.1.249	255.255.255.252
		2001:DB8:F:1::1/64	
	S0/0/1	172.16.1.253	255.255.255.252
		2001:DB8:F:2::1/64	
	Lo0	209.165.201.1	255.255.255.252
		2001:DB8:F:F::1/64	
	Link-Local	FE80::2	
	Router ID	2.2.2.2	
B1	G0/0	10.10.8.1	255.255.254.0
		2001:DB8:1:3::1/64	
	G0/1	10.10.10.1	255.255.254.0
		2001:DB8:1:4::1/64	
	S0/0/0	172.16.1.250	255.255.255.252
		2001:DB8:F:1::2/64	
	S0/0/1	172.16.1.245	255.255.255.252
		2001:DB8:F::1/64	
	Link-Local	FE80::1	
	Router ID	1.1.1.1	

Device	Interface	Addressing Information	
B3	G0/0	10.10.12.1	255.255.255.0
		2001:DB8:1:5::1/64	
	G0/1	10.10.13.1	255.255.255.0
		2001:DB8:1:6::1/64	
	S0/0/0	172.16.1.246	255.255.255.252
		2001:DB8:F::2/64	
	S0/0/1	172.16.1.254	255.255.255.252
		2001:DB8:F:2::2/64	
	Link-Local	FE80::3	
	Router ID	3.3.3.3	

Document the most basic routing commands you could use to configure EIGRP for IPv4. Include the commands to configure the LAN interfaces as passive. The commands for all three routers are the same, except for the router ID configuration for each router.

Now, for each router, document the network commands you would configure if the policy stated that you must also configure the wildcard mask for each interface participating in the EIGRP routing domain.

Verifying EIGRP with IPv4

Before any updates can be sent or received by EIGRP, routers must establish adjacencies with their neighbors. EIGRP routers establish adjacencies with neighbor routers by exchanging EIGRP Hello packets.

Use the _____ command to view the neighbor table and verify that EIGRP has established an adjacency with its neighbors. This command enables you to verify and troubleshoot EIGRP. Example 7-1 shows the neighbor table for HQ.

Example 7-1   EIGRP Neighbor Table for HQ

```
HQ# _____

EIGRP-IPv4 Neighbors for AS(1)

H   Address            Interface           Hold Uptime    SRTT   RTO   Q   Seq
                                           (sec)          (ms)         Cnt Num
1   172.16.1.254       Se0/0/1             14 00:28:35    2      100   0   33
0   172.16.1.250       Se0/0/0             10 00:28:48    1      100   0   36
```

As with OSPF, you can use the _____ command shown in Example 7-2 to verify that EIGRP is enabled. Because this configuration was done on a router with IOS 15.1, automatic summarization is disabled by default.

Example 7-2   Verifying EIGRP Is Enabled on HQ

```
HQ# _____

*** IP Routing is NSF aware ***

Routing Protocol is "eigrp 1"
  Outgoing update filter list for all interfaces is not set
  Incoming update filter list for all interfaces is not set
  Default networks flagged in outgoing updates
  Default networks accepted from incoming updates
  EIGRP-IPv4 Protocol for AS(1)
    Metric weight K1=1, K2=0, K3=1, K4=0, K5=0
    NSF-aware route hold timer is 240
    Router-ID: 2.2.2.2
    Topology : 0 (base)
      Active Timer: 3 min
      Distance: internal 90 external 170
      Maximum path: 4
      Maximum hopcount 100
      Maximum metric variance 1


  Automatic Summarization: disabled
  Maximum path: 4
```

```
   Routing for Networks:
      10.10.0.0/22
      10.10.4.0/22
      172.16.1.248/30
      172.16.1.252/30
   Passive Interface(s):
      GigabitEthernet0/0
      GigabitEthernet0/1
   Routing Information Sources:
      Gateway          Distance        Last Update
      172.16.1.254           90        00:29:47
      172.16.1.250           90        00:29:47
   Distance: internal 90 external 170
```

Another way to verify that EIGRP and other functions of the router are configured properly is to examine the routing tables with the _____ command. EIGRP routes are denoted in the routing table with a _____, which stands for DUAL.

Example 7-3 shows output from the routing table for B1 with only the EIGRP routes shown. Also, notice that the output begins at the "Gateway of last resort is not set" statement. What command generated this output?

_____

Example 7-3   B1 Routing Table with EIGRP Routes

```
B1# _____
Gateway of last resort is not set


      10.0.0.0/8 is variably subnetted, 8 subnets, 4 masks
D        10.10.0.0/22 [90/2172416] via 172.16.1.249, 00:43:44, Serial0/0/0
D        10.10.4.0/22 [90/2172416] via 172.16.1.249, 00:43:44, Serial0/0/0
D        10.10.12.0/24 [90/2684416] via 172.16.1.249, 00:43:31, Serial0/0/0
D        10.10.13.0/24 [90/2684416] via 172.16.1.249, 00:43:31, Serial0/0/0
      172.16.0.0/16 is variably subnetted, 5 subnets, 2 masks
D     172.16.1.252/30 [90/2681856] via 172.16.1.246, 00:00:05, Serial0/0/1
B1#
```

Packet Tracer
☐ Activity

Lab - Configuring Basic EIGRP with IPv4 (SN 7.2.2.5/RP 4.2.2.5)

Packet Tracer - Configuring Basic EIGRP with IPv4 (SN 7.2.2.4/RP 4.2.2.4)

Operation of EIGRP

EIGRP uses the Diffusing Update Algorithm (DUAL) to select the best routes based on a composite metric. This section reviews the values of the EIGRP metric and how EIGRP performs the calculation to arrive at the metric displayed in the routing table.

EIGRP Metric Concepts

List the values EIGRP uses in its composite metric to calculate the preferred path to a network:

- ▪
- ▪
- ▪
- ▪

Record the formula used to calculate the *default* EIGRP composite metric.

What command can you use to change the default K values?

What command do you use to verify the K values used by EIGRP?

What command enables you to verify the actual values of the EIGRP metric?

The _____ metric is displayed in Kbit (kilobits). The WIC-2T and HWIC-2T use the default value of _____ bps, which is the value for a _____ connection. The value may or may not reflect the actual physical _____ of the interface. If actual _____ of the link differs from the default value, you should modify the value. We will review modifying the bandwidth calculation to reflect actual values in the next chapter.

_____ is a measure of the time it takes for a packet to traverse a route. This metric is a static value and is expressed in _____.

Complete Table 7-3.

Table 7-3   Interface Delay Values

Media	Delay
Ethernet	
Fast Ethernet	
Gigabit Ethernet	
FDDI	
T1 (serial default)	

Media	Delay
DS0 (64 Kbps)	
1024 Kbps	
56 Kbps	

_____ is based on the worst value on a particular link and is computed based on keepalives.

_____ is based on the worst value on a particular link and is computed based on packet rates.

However, because the EIGRP composite metric defaults to _____ and _____ only, _____ and _____ are not normally considered in the calculation of metric.

DUAL Concepts Exercise

Dual provides the following:

- _____ paths
- _____ backup paths which can be used immediately
- Fast _____
- Minimum _____ usage with _____ updates

Briefly explain the term *successor*.

Briefly explain what is meant by *feasible distance*.

Examine the following output for B1's routing table shown in Example 7-4.

Example 7-4   Feasible Distance and Successors in the B1 Routing Table

```
B1# show ip route eigrp | begin Gateway
Gateway of last resort is not set

     10.0.0.0/8 is variably subnetted, 8 subnets, 4 masks
D       10.10.0.0/22 [90/2172416] via 172.16.1.249, 03:06:49, Serial0/0/0
D       10.10.4.0/22 [90/2172416] via 172.16.1.249, 03:06:49, Serial0/0/0
D       10.10.12.0/24 [90/2684416] via 172.16.1.249, 03:06:49, Serial0/0/0
D       10.10.13.0/24 [90/2684416] via 172.16.1.249, 03:06:49, Serial0/0/0
     172.16.0.0/16 is variably subnetted, 5 subnets, 2 masks
D       172.16.1.252/30 [90/2681856] via 172.16.1.249, 03:06:50, Serial0/0/0
```

Answer the questions that follow:

What is the IP address of the successor for network 10.10.4.0/22?

What is the feasible distance to 10.10.4.0/22?

What is the IP address of the successor for network 10.10.12.0/24?

What is the feasible distance to 10.10.12.0/24?

Briefly explain the term *feasible successor*.

Briefly explain *feasibility condition*.

Briefly explain *reported distance*.

The successor, feasible distance, and any feasible successors with their reported distances are kept by a router in its EIGRP topology table or topology database. This table can be viewed using the _____ command, as shown in Example 7-5.

Example 7-5   Successors and Feasible Successors in the B1 Topology Table

```
B1# _____

EIGRP-IPv4 Topology Table for AS(1)/ID(1.1.1.1)

Codes: P - Passive, A - Active, U - Update, Q - Query, R - Reply,
       r - reply Status, s - sia Status


P 10.10.8.0/23, 1 successors, FD is 28160
        via Connected, GigabitEthernet0/0
P 172.16.1.248/30, 1 successors, FD is 2169856
        via Connected, Serial0/0/0
P 172.16.1.244/30, 1 successors, FD is 3845120
        via Connected, Serial0/0/1
P 10.10.12.0/24, 1 successors, FD is 2684416
        via 172.16.1.249 (2684416/2172416), Serial0/0/0
        via 172.16.1.246 (3847680/28160), Serial0/0/1
P 10.10.4.0/22, 1 successors, FD is 2172416
        via 172.16.1.249 (2172416/28160), Serial0/0/0
P 172.16.1.252/30, 1 successors, FD is 2681856
        via 172.16.1.249 (2681856/2169856), Serial0/0/0
        via 172.16.1.246 (4357120/2169856), Serial0/0/1
```

```
P 10.10.0.0/22, 1 successors, FD is 2172416
        via 172.16.1.249 (2172416/28160), Serial0/0/0
P 10.10.13.0/24, 1 successors, FD is 2684416
        via 172.16.1.249 (2684416/2172416), Serial0/0/0
        via 172.16.1.246 (3847680/28160), Serial0/0/1
P 10.10.10.0/23, 1 successors, FD is 28160
        via Connected, GigabitEthernet0/1
```

The topology table lists all successors and feasible successors that DUAL has calculated to destination networks. Use the partial output in Example 9-5 to answer the following questions:

For route 10.10.12.0/24...

What is the IP address of the successor?

What is the reported distance of the successor?

What is the feasible distance of the successor?

What is the IP address of the feasible successor?

What is the reported distance of the feasible successor?

What is the feasible distance of the feasible successor?

Notice that the reported distance of the feasible successor is less than the feasible distance of the successor.

What happens if an EIGRP router doesn't have feasible successor in the topology table and the router loses connection to the successor?

DUAL FSM Completion Exercise

A finite state machine (FSM) is an abstract machine, not a mechanical device with moving parts. FSMs define a set of possible states that something can go through, what events cause those states, and what events result from those states. Designers use FSMs to describe how a device, computer program, or routing algorithm will react to a set of input events.

Figure 7-7 is a simplified flowchart of DUAL's FSM. Fill in the flowchart with the states EIGRP moves through when it loses connectivity with a successor. The flowchart should serve as a visual study aid to help you remember how DUAL converges on new routes.

Figure 7-7   DUAL FSM Flowchart

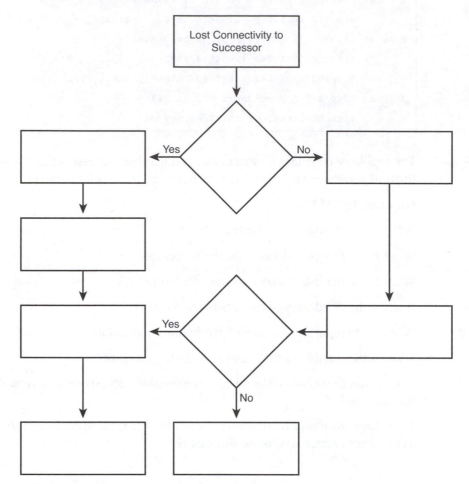

7.3.4.4 Packet Tracer - Investigating DUAL FSM

Configuring EIGRP for IPv6

EIGRP for IPv4 and EIGRP for IPv6 are almost identical in their operation. Configuring EIGRP for IPv6 is actually easier than IPv4. No need to configure network statements. Simply enable EIGRP for IPv6 globally, assigning a router ID. Then enable EIGRP on each interface you want to participate in the EIGRP routing process.

Comparing EIGRP for IPv4 and EIGRP for IPv6

In Table 7-4, indicate whether an EIGRP feature is associated with EIGRP for IPv4, EIGRP for IPv6, or both.

Table 7-4   Comparing EIGRP for IPv4 and IPv6

Features	EIGRP for IPv4	EIGRP for IPv6	Both
Advertised IPv4 networks			
Advertised IPv6 networks			
Distance vector			
DUAL algorithm			

Features	EIGRP for IPv4	EIGRP for IPv6	Both
Default metric: bandwidth and delay			
Transport protocol: RTP			
Incremental, partial, and bounded updates			
Neighbor discovery: Hello packets			
224.0.0.10 multicast			
FF02::10 multicast			

Configuring and Verifying EIGRP for IPv6

The steps to configure EIGRP for IPv6 are as follows:

Step 1. Enable IPv6 routing.

Step 2. Enable EIGRP for IPv6 globally and configure the router ID.

Step 3. Enable the interfaces that are to participate in EIGRP for IPv6.

With those steps in mind, document the configurations for each router shown in Figure 7-6.

What command enables you to verify adjacency with other EIGRP routers?

```
B1# _____
EIGRP-IPv6 Neighbors for AS(1)
H   Address              Interface         Hold Uptime   SRTT   RTO  Q   Seq
                                           (sec)         (ms)        Cnt Num
1   Link-local address:  Se0/0/1           11 00:14:52    1    186   0   50
    FE80::3
0   Link-local address:  Se0/0/0           12 00:14:53    1    100   0   25
    FE80::2
```

What command enables you to display the EIGRP parameters, including the K values, router ID, process ID, and administrative distances?

```
B1# _____
IPv6 Routing Protocol is "connected"
IPv6 Routing Protocol is "eigrp 1"
EIGRP-IPv6 Protocol for AS(1)
  Metric weight K1=1, K2=0, K3=1, K4=0, K5=0
  NSF-aware route hold timer is 240
  Router-ID: 1.1.1.1
  Topology : 0 (base)
    Active Timer: 3 min
    Distance: internal 90 external 170
    Maximum path: 16
    Maximum hopcount 100
    Maximum metric variance 1

  Interfaces:
    Serial0/0/0
    Serial0/0/1
    GigabitEthernet0/0
    GigabitEthernet0/1
  Redistribution:
    None
IPv6 Routing Protocol is "ND"
```

What command enables you to verify the EIGRP routes are installed in the routing table?

```
B1# _____
IPv6 Routing Table - default - 14 entries
Codes: C - Connected, L - Local, S - Static, U - Per-user Static route
       B - BGP, R - RIP, H - NHRP, I1 - ISIS L1
       I2 - ISIS L2, IA - ISIS interarea, IS - ISIS summary, D - EIGRP
       EX - EIGRP external, ND - ND Default, NDp - ND Prefix, DCE - Destination
       NDr - Redirect, O - OSPF Intra, OI - OSPF Inter, OE1 - OSPF ext 1
       OE2 - OSPF ext 2, ON1 - OSPF NSSA ext 1, ON2 - OSPF NSSA ext 2
```

```
D    2001:DB8:1:1::/64 [90/2172416]
        via FE80::2, Serial0/0/0
D    2001:DB8:1:2::/64 [90/2172416]
        via FE80::2, Serial0/0/0
D    2001:DB8:1:5::/64 [90/2684416]
        via FE80::2, Serial0/0/0
D    2001:DB8:1:6::/64 [90/2684416]
        via FE80::2, Serial0/0/0
D    2001:DB8:F:2::/64 [90/2681856]
        via FE80::2, Serial0/0/0
```

Lab - Configuring Basic EIGRP for IPv6 (SN 7.4.3.5/RP 4.4.3.5)

Packet Tracer - Configuring Basic EIGRP with IPv6 (SN 7.4.3.4/RP 4.4.3.5)

Packet Tracer
☐ Activity

CHAPTER 8

EIGRP Advanced Configurations and Troubleshooting

This chapter reviews the various ways you can adjust your Enhanced Interior Gateway Routing Protocol (EIGRP) implementation to provide additional capabilities and functionality. In addition, troubleshooting EIGRP is also covered.

Advanced EIGRP Configurations

Now that you are familiar with the basic configuration and verification commands for implementing EIGRP, this section focuses on ways you can tweak the implementation to improve performance, enable load balancing, and authenticate updates between EIGRP neighbors.

Automatic Summarization

Before Cisco IOS 15.01(1)M and 12.2(33), automatic summarization in EIGRP was enabled by default. Briefly explain the concept of automatic summarization.

Assume an EIGRP router is using automatic summarization. In Table 8-1, record the classful address advertised by the router for each listing of subnets.

Table 8-1   Determine the Classful Networks Advertised by an EIGRP Router

Subnets	Classful Networks
10.10.10.0/24, 10.10.11.0/24, 10.10.12.0/24	
172.16.16.0/22, 172.16.18.0/22	
192.168.1.0/25, 192.168.1.128/25, 192.168.2.0/25, 192.168.2.128/25	

EIGRP automatic summarization should be used only if you are absolutely sure that you do not have any discontiguous subnets. For example, in Figure 8-1, the addressing scheme is discontiguous.

Figure 8-1   EIGRP Automatic Summarization Topology with Discontiguous Subnets

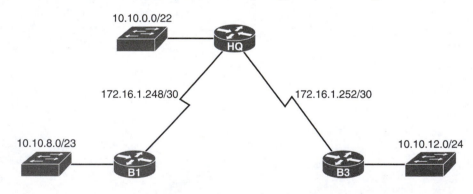

If you enable automatic summarization on the routers, they will not advertise the specific subnets that belong to 10.0.0.0/8 across the 172.16.0.0 WAN links. Instead, they automatically summarize the subnets to 10.0.0.0/8 and advertise the classful network. But each router already has a link in the 10.0.0.0/8 address space, so the update from the neighbor is stored in the topology table. No routes to the subnets are installed.

Automatic summarization is disabled by default in IOS 15 and later. What command including the router prompt will enable automatic summarization?

_____

You can verify whether automatic summarization is enabled with the _____ command displayed in Example 8-1 for HQ from Figure 8-1.

Example 8-1   Verifying Automatic Summarization Is in Effect

```
HQ# _____

*** IP Routing is NSF aware ***


Routing Protocol is "eigrp 1"
  Outgoing update filter list for all interfaces is not set
  Incoming update filter list for all interfaces is not set
  Default networks flagged in outgoing updates
  Default networks accepted from incoming updates
  EIGRP-IPv4 Protocol for AS(1)
    Metric weight K1=1, K2=0, K3=1, K4=0, K5=0
    NSF-aware route hold timer is 240
    Router-ID: 2.2.2.2
    Topology : 0 (base)
      Active Timer: 3 min
      Distance: internal 90 external 170
      Maximum path: 4
      Maximum hopcount 100
      Maximum metric variance 1

  Automatic Summarization: enabled
    172.16.0.0/16 for Gi0/0
      Summarizing 2 components with metric 2169856
    10.0.0.0/8 for Se0/0/0, Se0/0/1
      Summarizing 1 component with metric 28160
  Maximum path: 4
  Routing for Networks:
    10.0.0.0
    172.16.0.0
  Routing Information Sources:
    Gateway         Distance      Last Update
    172.16.1.254          90      00:01:30
    172.16.1.250          90      00:01:30
  Distance: internal 90 external 170
```

To view the entire EIGRP topology table for HQ, use the _____ command to generate the output displayed in Example 8-2.

Example 8-2   Viewing the Complete EIGRP Topology Table

```
HQ# _____
EIGRP-IPv4 Topology Table for AS(1)/ID(2.2.2.2)
Codes: P - Passive, A - Active, U - Update, Q - Query, R - Reply,
       r - reply Status, s - sia Status


P 172.16.1.248/30, 1 successors, FD is 2169856, serno 2
        via Connected, Serial0/0/0
P 172.16.0.0/16, 1 successors, FD is 2169856, serno 4
        via Summary (2169856/0), Null0
P 10.0.0.0/8, 1 successors, FD is 28160, serno 3
        via Summary (28160/0), Null0
        via 172.16.1.250 (2172416/28160), Serial0/0/0
        via 172.16.1.254 (2172416/28160), Serial0/0/1
P 172.16.1.252/30, 1 successors, FD is 2169856, serno 8
        via Connected, Serial0/0/1
P 10.10.0.0/22, 1 successors, FD is 28160, serno 1
        via Connected, GigabitEthernet0/0
```

You can see that HQ has a route for 10.0.0.0/8 from both B1 and B3 in its topology table. However, it also has its own summary route with a better metric. This is the route installed and used by HQ, as verified with the _____ command displayed in Example 8-3.

Example 8-3   Verifying the Summary Route Installed on HQ

```
HQ# _____
Gateway of last resort is not set

      10.0.0.0/8 is variably subnetted, 3 subnets, 3 masks
D        10.0.0.0/8 is a summary, 00:08:42, Null0
      172.16.0.0/16 is variably subnetted, 5 subnets, 3 masks
D        172.16.0.0/16 is a summary, 00:09:01, Null0
```

Briefly explain the purpose of the Null0 interface.

Manual Summarization

In EIGRP design scenarios where it is not desirable to prevent discontiguous subnets, you may still want to encourage scalable designs so that you can take advantage of EIGRP's manual summarization. This will help reduce the size of routing tables.

IPv4 Manual Summarization

Figure 8-2 shows the same EIGRP topology we used in Chapter 7, "EIGRP." However, now the topology shows the contracted bandwidth rates on each of the serial interfaces. We will use that information later to tune how EIGRP chooses the best route.

Note: The bandwidths shown in Figure 8-2 are not realistic for today's network implementations that require gigabit speeds across WAN links. These bandwidths are used for simplicity.

Figure 8-2   Dual-Stack EIGRP Topology with Bandwidths

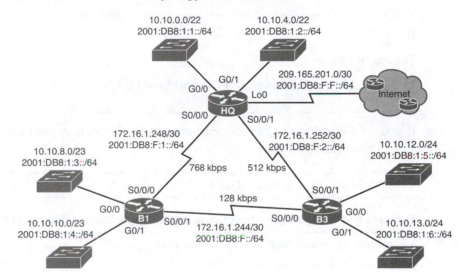

To calculate the IPv4 summary routes, use the same technique you used to calculate a IPv4 static summary routes:

Step 1.   Write out the networks to be summarized in binary.

Step 2.   To find the subnet mask for summarization, start with the far-left bit.

Step 3.   Working from left to right, find all the bits that match consecutively.

Step 4.   When there is a column of bits that do not match, stop. This is the summary boundary.

Step 5.   Count the number of far-left matching bits, which in this example is 22. This number is used to determine the subnet mask for the summarized route: /22 or 255.255.252.0.

Step 6.   To find the network address for summarization, copy the matching 22 bits and add all 0 bits to the end to make 32 bits.

Once you have your summary, configure the desired interfaces with the **ip summary-address eigrp** command. Each interface that will send out an EIGRP update should have the command.

In Figure 8-2, each router can summarizes the two local LANs into one summary route. Calculate the summary routes for each route and record the commands to configure the serial interfaces.

HQ

Summary Route: _____

Command to configure Serial 0/0/0 and Serial 0/0/1:

_____

B1

Summary Route: _____

Command to configure Serial 0/0/0 and Serial 0/0/1:

_____

B3

Summary Route: _____

Command to configure Serial 0/0/0 and Serial 0/0/1:

_____

If you are following along in a simulator or on lab equipment, your EIGRP routing tables should look like Example 8-4.

Note: We have not yet configured the bandwidth values shown in Figure 8-2.

Example 8-4   EIGRP Routing Tables with Manual Summarization in Effect

```
HQ# show ip route eigrp | begin Gateway
Gateway of last resort is not set


     10.0.0.0/8 is variably subnetted, 7 subnets, 4 masks
D        10.10.0.0/21 is a summary, 00:06:50, Null0
D        10.10.8.0/22 [90/2172416] via 172.16.1.250, 00:01:43, Serial0/0/0
D        10.10.12.0/23 [90/2172416] via 172.16.1.254, 00:01:13, Serial0/0/1
     172.16.0.0/16 is variably subnetted, 5 subnets, 2 masks
D        172.16.1.244/30 [90/2681856] via 172.16.1.254, 00:01:43, Serial0/0/1
                         [90/2681856] via 172.16.1.250, 00:01:43, Serial0/0/0
B1# show ip route eigrp | begin Gateway
Gateway of last resort is not set


     10.0.0.0/8 is variably subnetted, 7 subnets, 4 masks
D        10.10.0.0/21 [90/2172416] via 172.16.1.249, 00:00:54, Serial0/0/0
D        10.10.8.0/22 is a summary, 00:06:21, Null0
D        10.10.12.0/23 [90/2172416] via 172.16.1.246, 00:00:54, Serial0/0/1
     172.16.0.0/16 is variably subnetted, 5 subnets, 2 masks
D        172.16.1.252/30 [90/2681856] via 172.16.1.249, 00:00:54, Serial0/0/0
                         [90/2681856] via 172.16.1.246, 00:00:54, Serial0/0/1
B3# show ip route eigrp | begin Gateway
Gateway of last resort is not set
```

```
       10.0.0.0/8 is variably subnetted, 7 subnets, 5 masks
D         10.10.0.0/21 [90/2172416] via 172.16.1.253, 00:00:48, Serial0/0/1
D         10.10.8.0/22 [90/2172416] via 172.16.1.245, 00:00:48, Serial0/0/0
D         10.10.12.0/23 is a summary, 00:00:19, Null0
       172.16.0.0/16 is variably subnetted, 5 subnets, 2 masks
D         172.16.1.248/30 [90/2681856] via 172.16.1.253, 00:00:48, Serial0/0/1
                           [90/2681856] via 172.16.1.245, 00:00:48, Serial0/0/0
```

IPv6 Manual Summarization

Briefly explain why IPv6 does not support automatic summarization.

You can manually configure IPv6 summary routes. However, the IPv6 addressing in Figure 8-2 was not designed for summary routes. If you summarized the IPv6 LANs on any of the routers, you would be including IPv6 LANs from one or both of the other routers.

For example, the summary for the IPv6 LANs on B3 would be 2001:DB8:1:4::/62. The calculation focuses on the fourth hextet since it is the one that is changing:

```
0000 0000 0000 0100 --> included in summary (B1 LAN)

0000 0000 0000 0101 --> B3 LAN

0000 0000 0000 0110 --> B3 LAN

0000 0000 0000 0111 --> included in a B1 summary, if configured
```

You can see that this summary would include the B1 IPv6 LAN, 2001:DB8:1:4::/64. But it would also include additional address space summarized by B1 if B1 also configured an IPv6 manual summary route. In fact, a summary route on B1 would include all the IPv6 LANs in the topology. Prove this using the following workspace to calculate what the IPv6 summary route would be for B1.

```
0000 0000 0000 0_____

0000 0000 0000 0_____

0000 0000 0000 0_____

0000 0000 0000 0_____

0000 0000 0000 0_____

0000 0000 0000 0_____

0000 0000 0000 0_____

0000 0000 0000 0_____
```

What would be the summary route for B1?

| Packet Tracer ☐ Activity | **Packet Tracer - Configuring EIGRP Manual Summary Routes for IPv4 and IPv6 (SN 8.1.2.5/RP 5.1.2.5)** |

Default Route Propagation

Propagating a default route in EIGRP requires one additional command in your EIGRP configuration. What is the command, including the router prompt, for both IPv4 and IPv6?

IPv4:

IPv6:

Figure 8-2 is using a Loopback interface to simulate a connection to the Internet. Record the commands to configure an IPv4 default route, IPv6 default route, and redistribute the routes to B1 and B3.

If you are following along in a simulator or on lab equipment, your verification output for B1 and B3 should look like Example 8-5.

Example 8-5   EIGRP Routing Tables with Default Route Propagation

```
B1# show ip route eigrp | begin Gateway
Gateway of last resort is 172.16.1.249 to network 0.0.0.0


D*EX  0.0.0.0/0 [170/2297856] via 172.16.1.249, 00:12:58, Serial0/0/0
        10.0.0.0/8 is variably subnetted, 7 subnets, 4 masks
D        10.10.0.0/21 [90/2172416] via 172.16.1.249, 06:04:19, Serial0/0/0
D        10.10.8.0/22 is a summary, 00:05:31, Null0
D        10.10.12.0/23 [90/2172416] via 172.16.1.246, 06:04:19, Serial0/0/1
        172.16.0.0/16 is variably subnetted, 5 subnets, 2 masks
D        172.16.1.252/30 [90/2681856] via 172.16.1.249, 06:04:19, Serial0/0/0
                         [90/2681856] via 172.16.1.246, 06:04:19, Serial0/0/1
B1# show ipv6 route eigrp | begin EX  ::/0
EX  ::/0 [170/2169856]
     via FE80::2, Serial0/0/0
D   2001:DB8:1:1::/64 [90/2172416]
     via FE80::2, Serial0/0/0
```

```
D    2001:DB8:1:2::/64 [90/2172416]
      via FE80::2, Serial0/0/0
D    2001:DB8:1:6::/64 [90/2172416]
      via FE80::3, Serial0/0/1
D    2001:DB8:F:2::/64 [90/2681856]
      via FE80::2, Serial0/0/0
      via FE80::3, Serial0/0/1
B1# ping 209.165.201.1
Type escape sequence to abort.
Sending 5, 100-byte ICMP Echos to 209.165.201.1, timeout is 2 seconds:
!!!!!
Success rate is 100 percent (5/5), round-trip min/avg/max = 1/1/4 ms
B1# ping 2001:db8:f:f::1
Type escape sequence to abort.
Sending 5, 100-byte ICMP Echos to 2001:DB8:F:F::1, timeout is 2 seconds:
!!!!!
Success rate is 100 percent (5/5), round-trip min/avg/max = 1/1/4 ms
B3# show ip route eigrp | begin Gateway
Gateway of last resort is 172.16.1.253 to network 0.0.0.0


D*EX  0.0.0.0/0 [170/2297856] via 172.16.1.253, 00:13:32, Serial0/0/1
        10.0.0.0/8 is variably subnetted, 7 subnets, 5 masks
D         10.10.0.0/21 [90/2172416] via 172.16.1.253, 06:04:52, Serial0/0/1
D         10.10.8.0/22 [90/2172416] via 172.16.1.245, 06:04:52, Serial0/0/0
D         10.10.12.0/23 is a summary, 06:05:05, Null0
        172.16.0.0/16 is variably subnetted, 5 subnets, 2 masks
D         172.16.1.248/30 [90/2681856] via 172.16.1.253, 06:04:52, Serial0/0/1
                          [90/2681856] via 172.16.1.245, 06:04:52, Serial0/0/0
B3# show ipv6 route eigrp | begin EX   ::/0
EX   ::/0 [170/2169856]
      via FE80::2, Serial0/0/1
D    2001:DB8:1:1::/64 [90/2172416]
      via FE80::2, Serial0/0/1
D    2001:DB8:1:2::/64 [90/2172416]
      via FE80::2, Serial0/0/1
D    2001:DB8:1:4::/64 [90/2172416]
      via FE80::1, Serial0/0/0
D    2001:DB8:F:1::/64 [90/2681856]
      via FE80::1, Serial0/0/0
      via FE80::2, Serial0/0/1
B3# ping 209.165.201.1
Type escape sequence to abort.
```

```
Sending 5, 100-byte ICMP Echos to 209.165.201.1, timeout is 2 seconds:
!!!!!
Success rate is 100 percent (5/5), round-trip min/avg/max = 1/2/4 ms
B3# ping 2001:db8:f:f::1
Type escape sequence to abort.
Sending 5, 100-byte ICMP Echos to 2001:DB8:F:F::1, timeout is 2 seconds:
!!!!!
Success rate is 100 percent (5/5), round-trip min/avg/max = 1/1/4 ms
```

8.1.3.4 Packet Tracer - Propagating a Default Route in EIGRP for IPv4 and IPv6

Fine-Tuning EIGRP Interfaces

Bandwidth Utilization

By default, EIGRP will use only up to _____ percent of the bandwidth of an interface for EIGRP information. This prevents the EIGRP process from overutilizing a link and not allowing enough bandwidth for the routing of normal traffic.

The _____ command can be used to configure the percentage of bandwidth that may be used by EIGRP on an interface. Record the full syntax for this command.

This command uses the amount of configured bandwidth (or the default bandwidth) when calculating the percent that EIGRP can use.

Hello Intervals and Holdtimes

Hello intervals and holdtimes are configurable on a per-interface basis and do not have to match with other EIGRP routers to establish adjacencies.

Record the command to configure a different Hello interval.

If you change the Hello interval, make sure that you also change the holdtime to a value equal to or greater than the Hello interval. Otherwise, neighbor adjacency will go down after the holdtime expires and before the next Hello interval.

Record the command to configure a different holdtime.

EIGRP has different default Hello intervals and holdtimes based on the type of link. Complete Table 8-2 with the default values.

Table 8-2   Default Hello Intervals and Holdtimer for EIGRP

Bandwidth	Example Link	Default Hello Interval	Default Holdtime
1.544 Mbps	Multipoint Frame Relay		
Greater Than 1.544 Mbps	T1, Ethernet		

Load Balancing

Briefly describe equal-cost load balancing.

By default, EIGRP uses up to _____ equal-cost paths to load balance traffic. You can see load balancing in effect in the routing tables shown in previous Examples 8-4 and 8-5.

The reason EIGRP is load balancing is that we have not configured the actual bandwidth shown in Figure 8-2.

Record the commands to configure the routers with the correct bandwidth values.

Once the routers are properly configured with the actual bandwidth values, EIGRP recalculates the metrics and installs the best route in the routing table, as shown in Example 8-6. Notice that B1 and B3 are no longer using the 128-Kbps link to route to each other's LANs. Instead, they are each using the faster path through HQ.

Example 8-6   EIGRP Routing Tables After Bandwidth Configuration

```
B1# show ip route eigrp | begin Gateway
Gateway of last resort is 172.16.1.249 to network 0.0.0.0

D*EX  0.0.0.0/0 [170/3973120] via 172.16.1.249, 00:05:50, Serial0/0/0
      10.0.0.0/8 is variably subnetted, 7 subnets, 4 masks
D        10.10.0.0/21 [90/3847680] via 172.16.1.249, 00:05:50, Serial0/0/0
D        10.10.8.0/22 is a summary, 00:05:21, Null0
D        10.10.12.0/23 [90/6026496] via 172.16.1.249, 00:05:21, Serial0/0/0
      172.16.0.0/16 is variably subnetted, 5 subnets, 2 masks
D        172.16.1.252/30 [90/6023936] via 172.16.1.249, 00:05:31, Serial0/0/0
B1# show ipv6 route eigrp | begin EX  ::/0
EX  ::/0 [170/3845120]
     via FE80::2, Serial0/0/0
D   2001:DB8:1:1::/64 [90/3847680]
     via FE80::2, Serial0/0/0
```

```
D    2001:DB8:1:2::/64 [90/3847680]
       via FE80::2, Serial0/0/0
D    2001:DB8:1:6::/64 [90/6026496]
       via FE80::2, Serial0/0/0
D    2001:DB8:F:2::/64 [90/6023936]
       via FE80::2, Serial0/0/0
```

```
B3# show ip route eigrp | begin Gateway
Gateway of last resort is 172.16.1.253 to network 0.0.0.0


D*EX  0.0.0.0/0 [170/5639936] via 172.16.1.253, 00:05:43, Serial0/0/1
       10.0.0.0/8 is variably subnetted, 7 subnets, 5 masks
D         10.10.0.0/21 [90/5514496] via 172.16.1.253, 00:05:43, Serial0/0/1
D         10.10.8.0/22 [90/6026496] via 172.16.1.253, 00:05:43, Serial0/0/1
D         10.10.12.0/23 is a summary, 00:06:11, Null0
       172.16.0.0/16 is variably subnetted, 5 subnets, 2 masks
D         172.16.1.248/30 [90/6023936] via 172.16.1.253, 00:05:43, Serial0/0/1
B3# show ipv6 route eigrp | begin EX  ::/0
EX   ::/0 [170/5511936]
       via FE80::2, Serial0/0/1
D    2001:DB8:1:1::/64 [90/5514496]
       via FE80::2, Serial0/0/1
D    2001:DB8:1:2::/64 [90/5514496]
       via FE80::2, Serial0/0/1
D    2001:DB8:1:4::/64 [90/6026496]
       via FE80::2, Serial0/0/1
D    2001:DB8:F:1::/64 [90/6023936]
       via FE80::2, Serial0/0/1
```

Securing EIGRP Routing Updates

In most production networks, you would want to configure the EIGRP routers to authenticate updates received from neighbors. The steps to configure EIGRP with MD5 authentication are as follows:

Step 1.   Create a keychain and key.

Record the command syntax including the router prompt to configure a keychain and key.

Step 2.   Configure EIGRP authentication to use the keychain and key.

Record the command syntax, including the router prompt, to configure EIGRP authentication using the keychain and key.

Now record the commands to configure HQ to authenticate updates from B1 and B3. Assume that B1 and B3 are already configured. Use MYKEY as the keychain name, 1 as the key ID, and cisco123 as the key string.

Use the _____ command as displayed in Example 8-7 to verify that HQ has reestablished adjacency with B1 and B3.

Example 8-7   Verifying EIGRP Authentication

```
HQ# _____

EIGRP-IPv4 Neighbors for AS(1)

H   Address              Interface            Hold Uptime   SRTT   RTO  Q   Seq
                                              (sec)         (ms)        Cnt Num
1   172.16.1.250         Se0/0/0               10 00:06:25    2    192  0   59
0   172.16.1.254         Se0/0/1               13 00:07:09    3    288  0   59
```

 Lab - Configuring Advanced EIGRP for IPv4 Features (SN 8.1.5.5/RP 5.1.5.5)

Troubleshoot EIGRP

This section reviews the tools and procedures to troubleshoot EIGRP issues.

Commands for Troubleshooting EIGRP

In Table 8-3, the IPv4 version of the troubleshooting commands for EIGRP are listed. The same commands are available for IPv6. Indicate which command or commands you would use to answer each of the questions.

Table 8-3   Diagnosing EIGRP Connectivity Issues

Command	Is the Neighbor Table Correct?	Is the Routing Table Correct?	Does Traffic Take the Desired Path?
show ip eigrp neighbors			
show ip interface brief			
show ip eigrp interface			
show ip protocols			
show ip route eigrp			

Troubleshoot EIGRP Connectivity Issues

Using the configuration for the devices in Figure 8-2 and the following command outputs diagnose the EIGRP connectivity issue and recommend a solution.

Connectivity Issue #1

HQ and B1 have not formed a neighbor adjacency. Use the output in Example 8-8 to troubleshoot the first issue.

Example 8-8   Troubleshooting Command Output for Issue #1

```
HQ# show ip eigrp neighbors
EIGRP-IPv4 Neighbors for AS(1)
H   Address                 Interface        Hold Uptime   SRTT   RTO  Q   Seq
                                             (sec)         (ms)        Cnt Num
0   172.16.1.254            Se0/0/1           10 00:23:18    1    288  0   65
HQ# show ip interface brief
Interface               IP-Address       OK? Method Status               Protocol
Embedded-Service-Engine0/0 unassigned    YES unset  administratively down down
GigabitEthernet0/0      10.10.0.1        YES manual up                   up
GigabitEthernet0/1      10.10.4.1        YES manual up                   up
Serial0/0/0             172.16.1.250     YES manual up                   up
Serial0/0/1             172.16.1.253     YES manual up                   up
Loopback0               209.165.201.1    YES manual up                   up

B1# show ip eigrp neighbors
EIGRP-IPv4 Neighbors for AS(1)
H   Address                 Interface        Hold Uptime   SRTT   RTO  Q   Seq
                                             (sec)         (ms)        Cnt Num
1   172.16.1.246            Se0/0/1           12 00:26:47    9   1170  0   67
B1# show ip interface brief
Interface               IP-Address       OK? Method Status               Protocol
Embedded-Service-Engine0/0 unassigned    YES unset  administratively down down
GigabitEthernet0/0      10.10.8.1        YES manual up                   up
GigabitEthernet0/1      10.10.10.1       YES manual up                   up
Serial0/0/0             172.16.1.250     YES manual up                   up
Serial0/0/1             172.16.1.245     YES manual up                   up
```

Problem and Solution:

Connectivity Issue #2

HQ and B3 have not formed a neighbor adjacency. Example 8-9 displays the output for the second issue.

Example 8-9   Troubleshooting Command Output for Issue #2

```
HQ# show ipv6 eigrp neighbors
EIGRP-IPv6 Neighbors for AS(1)
H    Address                  Interface        Hold Uptime    SRTT   RTO  Q  Seq
                                               (sec)          (ms)       Cnt Num
0    Link-local address:      Se0/0/0          14 05:12:49     1    186  0  57
     FE80::1
B3# show ipv6 eigrp neighbors
EIGRP-IPv6 Neighbors for AS(2)
```

Problem and Solution:

Connectivity Issue #3

Although the IPv6 routes look correct, B3 is using a less-than-optimal route to reach the B1 and HQ IPv4 LANs. Use the output in Example 8-10 to troubleshoot the third issue.

Example 8-10   Troubleshooting Command Output for Issue #3

```
HQ# show ip protocols
*** IP Routing is NSF aware ***

Routing Protocol is "eigrp 1"
  Outgoing update filter list for all interfaces is not set
  Incoming update filter list for all interfaces is not set
  Default networks flagged in outgoing updates
  Default networks accepted from incoming updates
  Redistributing: static
  EIGRP-IPv4 Protocol for AS(1)
    Metric weight K1=1, K2=0, K3=1, K4=0, K5=0
    NSF-aware route hold timer is 240
    Router-ID: 2.2.2.2
    Topology : 0 (base)
      Active Timer: 3 min
```

```
                  Distance: internal 90 external 170

                  Maximum path: 4

                  Maximum hopcount 100

                  Maximum metric variance 1


          Automatic Summarization: disabled
          Address Summarization:

             10.10.0.0/21 for Se0/0/0, Se0/0/1

                Summarizing 2 components with metric 28160

          Maximum path: 4

          Routing for Networks:

             10.0.0.0

             172.16.0.0

          Passive Interface(s):

             GigabitEthernet0/0

             GigabitEthernet0/1

             Serial0/0/1

          Routing Information Sources:

             Gateway          Distance        Last Update

             172.16.1.254            90        00:17:55

             172.16.1.250            90        00:00:41

          Distance: internal 90 external 170
```

B3# **show ip route eigrp | begin Gateway**

```
Gateway of last resort is 172.16.1.245 to network 0.0.0.0


D*EX  0.0.0.0/0 [170/21152000] via 172.16.1.245, 00:08:32, Serial0/0/0

         10.0.0.0/8 is variably subnetted, 7 subnets, 5 masks

D        10.10.0.0/21 [90/21026560] via 172.16.1.245, 00:08:32, Serial0/0/0

D        10.10.8.0/22 [90/20514560] via 172.16.1.245, 00:08:32, Serial0/0/0

D        10.10.12.0/23 is a summary, 04:39:57, Null0

         172.16.0.0/16 is variably subnetted, 5 subnets, 2 masks

D        172.16.1.248/30 [90/21024000] via 172.16.1.245, 00:08:32, Serial0/0/0
```

B3# **show ipv6 route eigrp | begin EX ::/0**

```
EX   ::/0 [170/5511936]

     via FE80::2, Serial0/0/1

D    2001:DB8:1:1::/64 [90/5514496]

     via FE80::2, Serial0/0/1

D    2001:DB8:1:2::/64 [90/5514496]

     via FE80::2, Serial0/0/1

D    2001:DB8:1:4::/64 [90/6026496]

     via FE80::2, Serial0/0/1

D    2001:DB8:F:1::/64 [90/6023936]

     via FE80::2, Serial0/0/1
```

Problem and Solution:

Lab - Troubleshooting Basic EIGRP for IPv4 and IPv6 (SN 8.2.3.6/RP 5.2.3.6)

Lab - Troubleshooting Advanced EIGRP (SN 8.2.3.7/RP 5.2.3.7)

Packet Tracer - Troubleshooting EIGRP for IPv4 (SN 8.2.3.5/RP 5.2.3.5)

Packet Tracer - Skills Integration Challenge (SN 8.3.1.2/RP 5.3.1.2)

CHAPTER 9

IOS Images and Licensing

Network administrators are responsible for managing the routers and switches owned by the organization. This responsibility includes backing up and upgrading software images when needed. This chapter reviews basic IOS image concepts and management tasks.

Managing IOS System Files

Cisco IOS software is a sophisticated operating system that includes multiple release versions that are organized into software release families and software trains.

IOS Families, Trains, and Naming Conventions

A software release family is comprised of multiple IOS software release versions. What are the three features that distinguish an IOS software release family?

-
-
-

What are some major software releases within the software release family?

Briefly describe a software train.

The Cisco IOS Software 12.4 train is considered the _____ train, which receives mostly software (bug) fixes with the goal of increasing software quality. These releases are also designated as _____ releases (MD).

A _____ train is always associated with a _____ train (T train). A T train, such as 12.4T, receives the same software bug fixes as the _____ train.

What else does a T train include?

_____

T train releases are considered _____ (ED) releases.

Decoding the IOS release numbering conventions will go a long way in helping you understand the various trains used in the IOS 12.4 software release family. In Figure 9-1, indicate whether the release is a mainline train or a technology train. Then fill in the blanks for each part of the IOS 12 software release numbering scheme.

Releases before IOS 15 consisted of eight packages for Cisco routers. These packages were the following:

Five nonpremium packages:

- _____ : Entry-level Cisco IOS Software Image
- _____ : Converged voice and data, VoIP, VoFR, and IP Telephony
- _____ : Security and VPN features, including Cisco IOS Firewall, IDS/IPS, IPsec, 3DES, and VPN
- _____ : Adds SSH/SSL, ATM, VoATM, and MPLS to IP Voice
- _____ : Includes AppleTalk, IPX, and IBM Support

Figure 9-1   The IOS 12.4 Software Release Numbering Convention

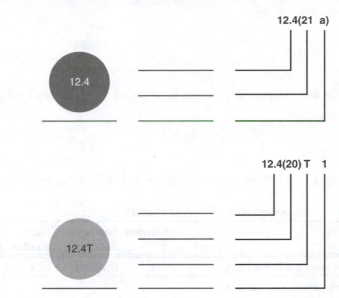

Three premium packages:

- _____ : Full Cisco IOS software features

- _____ : Enterprise base and service provider services

- _____ : Advanced security, service provider services, and support for IPv6

How does the Cisco IOS 15.0 release model differ from the mainline and T trains of 12.4?

In Figure 9-2, indicate whether the release is a mainline train or a technology train. Then fill in the blanks for each part of the IOS 15 software release numbering scheme.

Figure 9-2   The IOS 15 Software Release Numbering Convention

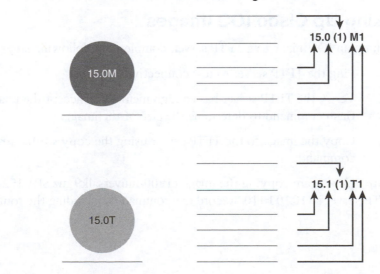

Briefly explain how Services on Demand for Cisco Integrated Services Routers Generation Two (ISR G2) works.

What is the key difference between universalk9 and universalk9_npe IOS images?

Decode the IOS 12 image name in Table 9-1. The first one is done for you.

Table 9-1   Decoding IOS 12 Image Names

IOS Images	Hardware	Feature Set	Train Number	Maintenance Release	Train Identifier	Rebuild Identifier
c1841-ipbasek9-mz.124-12.bin	1841	Ipbasek9	12.4	12	M	
c1841-advipservicesk9-mz.124-10b.bin						
c3725-entbase-mz.124-6.T.bin						

Decode the IOS 15 image name in Table 9-2. The first one is done for you.

Table 9-2   Decoding IOS 15 Image Names

IOS Images	Hardware	Feature Set	Major Release	Minor Release	New Feature Release	Maintenance Release	Maintenance Rebuild
c1900-universalk9-mz.SPA.153-2.T.bin	1900	Universal	15	3	2	T	
c2900-universalk9-mz.SPA.153-3.M.bin							
c1841-advipservicesk9-mz.151-4.M6.bin							6

Backing Up Cisco IOS Images

To back up an IOS image to a TFTP server, complete the following steps:

Step 1.   Ping the TFTP server to test connectivity.

Step 2.   Verify the TFTP server has enough memory to accept the image file. Use the **show flash** command to determine the size of the image.

Step 3.   Copy the image to the TFTP server using the **copy** *source-url destination-url* command.

In Figure 9-3, you are copying the image c1900-universalk9-mz.SPA.152-4.M1.bin from RTA to the TFTP server at 10.10.10.10. Record the commands, including the router prompt, to complete this task.

Figure 9-3   Backing Up an IOS to a TFTP Server

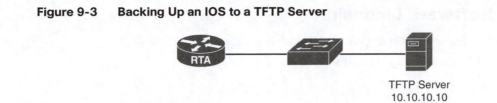

TFTP Server
10.10.10.10

Packet Tracer - Using a TFTP Server to Upgrade a Cisco IOS Image (SN 9.1.2.5/RP 10.1.2.5)

Packet Tracer
☐ **Activity**

Video Demonstration - Managing Cisco IOS Images (SN 9.1.2.6/RP 10.1.2.6)

☐ Video
Demonstration

IOS Licensing

Before Cisco IOS Software Release 15.0, your router came with the IOS already installed for the features you desired. If you wanted to upgrade the feature set, you had to order, download, and install a new version. That all changed with 15.0. Each device ships with the same universal image. You enable the features you need through the use of licensing keys.

Software Licensing

The feature sets that you enable with licensing keys are called _____. What are the four _____ available?

On which Cisco ISR G2 platforms can these licenses be used?

What command enables you to view the licenses currently supported on the router?

What are the three major steps to activate a new software package or feature on the router?

What two things are needed to obtain a license?

How is the UDI constructed?

What command displays the UDI?

What command installs the license?

License Verification and Management

After installing a license, you must reboot the router before the technology package is active and ready to use.

What two commands are used in Example 9-1 to verify the licenses installed?

Example 9-1   Verifying License Installation

```
Router# _____ | begin License Info:
License Info:


License UDI:
```

```
-------------------------------------------------
Device#    PID                 SN
-------------------------------------------------

*0         CISCO1941/K9        FTX163283RZ




Technology Package License Information for Module:'c1900'


--------------------------------------------------------------

Technology      Technology-package          Technology-package
                Current      Type           Next reboot
--------------------------------------------------------------

ipbase          ipbasek9     Permanent      ipbasek9
security        securityk9   EvalRightToUse securityk9
data            None         None           None


Configuration register is 0x2102


Router#
Index 1 Feature: ipbasek9
        Period left: Life time
        License Type: Permanent
        License State: Active, In Use
        License Count: Non-Counted
        License Priority: Medium
Index 2 Feature: securityk9
        Period left: 8  weeks 1  day
        Period Used: 2  days 0  hour
        License Type: EvalRightToUse
        License State: Active, In Use
        License Count: Non-Counted
        License Priority: Low
Index 3 Feature: datak9
        Period left: Not Activated
        Period Used: 0  minute  0  second
        License Type: EvalRightToUse
        License State: Not in Use, EULA not accepted
        License Count: Non-Counted
        License Priority: None
<output omitted>
```

In Example 9-1, the datak9 technology package is not in use. Record the commands, including the router prompt, to accept the EULA and activate the datak9 package.

What message do you receive when activate a package?

To back up your license files, save them to flash. Record the command, including the router prompt, to save the license files to flash.

Complete the following steps to uninstall a license:

Step 1.   Disable the technology package. Record the command, including the router prompt, to disable the datak9 technology package.

Step 2.   After reloading the router, clear the license from storage. Record the commands, including the router prompt, to clear the datak9 technology package.

Packet Tracer
☐ Activity

Packet Tracer - EIGRP Capstone (SN 9.3.1.2/RP 10.3.1.2)

Packet Tracer - OSPF Capstone (SN 9.3.1.3/RP 10.3.1.3)

Packet Tracer - Skills Integration Challenge (SN 9.3.1.4/RP 10.3.1.4)

☐ Video
Demonstration

Video Demonstration - Working with IOS 15 Image Licenses (SN 9.2.2.5/RP 10.2.2.5)

CHAPTER 10

Hierarchical Network Design

Part of your job as a network administrator is understanding how to build networks that are flexible, resilient, and manageable. Even if your direct responsibilities do not include actually designing the network, you still need a firm grasp of the benefits incurred from using a systematic design approach.

Hierarchical Network Design Overview

Networks come in all sizes. The size of the network is directly proportional to the complexity of the design. However, structured engineering principles can help guide the designer in formulating a plan even for the most complex networks.

Enterprise Network Campus Design

What are the three main categories of network sizes and how are they distinguished?

In Table 10-1, indicate the structured engineering principle that is best described by the characteristic.

Table 10-1   Structured Engineering Principles

Characteristic	Hierarchy	Modularity	Resiliency	Flexibility
Is available to users regardless of the current conditions				
High-level tool for designing a reliable network				
Can be easily modified				
Examples include the data center and the Internet edge				

Hierarchical Network Design

Briefly describe the three layers of the hierarchical network design.

- Access layer:

- Distribution layer:

- Core layer:

In Table 10-2, indicate the layer that is best described by the function

Table 10-2   Hierarchical Network Layer Functions

Layer Function	Access	Distribution	Core
Highest speed switching of the three layers			
Policy-based security			
Port security			
Redundancy and load balancing			
Broadcast domain control			
Spanning tree			

Layer Function	Access	Distribution	Core
Layer 2 switching			
Avoid CPU-intensive packet manipulation			
Aggregates traffic from distribution devices			
Aggregating LAN and WAN links			

Briefly explain the concept of a collapsed core.

Cisco Enterprise Architecture

Hierarchical network design is fine for campus network implementations. But the networks for many organizations span larger areas than just a campus to include teleworkers, branch sites, and data centers. These networks call for design approach where functions can be separated into modules.

Modular Network Design

Briefly describe three benefits for using a modular approach to network design.

In Table 10-3, indicate which module is described by the feature.

Table 10-3   Features of Modules in the Enterprise Architecture

Module Feature	Access-Distribution	Services	Data Center	Enterprise Edge
Provides resources necessary to employees so that they can effectively create, collaborate, and interact				
Could include wireless controls, policy gateways, and unified communications services				
Fundamental component of a campus design				
Consists of the Internet Edge and WAN Edge				
Provide connectivity outside the enterprise				
Originally called the server farm				

In Figure 10-1, label the modules of the Enterprise Architecture.

Figure 10-1   Identify Modules of the Enterprise Architecture

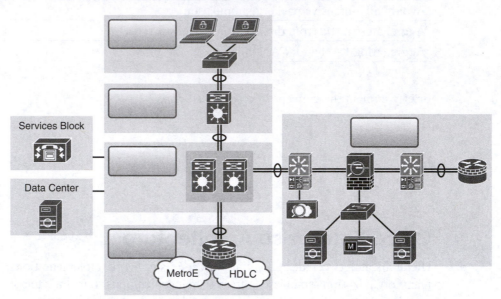

Cisco Enterprise Architecture Model

What are the three primary modules of the Cisco Enterprise Architecture model?

Which module provides connectivity to the data center, branches, and teleworkers?

What are the submodules of the Enterprise Campus module?

What are the submodules of the Enterprise Edge module?

What is the main purpose of the Service Provider Edge module?

In Table 10-4, indicate the service provider solution described.

Table 10-4   Service Provider Designs

Service Provider Connectivity Solution	Single-Homed	Dual-Homed	Multihomed	Dual-Multihomed
Connections to 2 or more ISPs				
A single connection to 1 ISP				
Multiple connections to 2 or more ISPs				
2 or more connections to 1 ISP				

What are the submodules of the remote module?

In Table 10-5, indicate which module is best described by the function.

Table 10-5   Cisco Enterprise Architecture Model Functions

Cisco Enterprise Architecture Feature	Enterprise Campus	Enterprise Edge	Service Provider Edge	Remote
Aggregates connectivity from various functional areas.				
Allows employees to work at non-campus locations.				
Provides cost-effective access across large geographic areas.				
Could use high-end Cisco Catalyst switches or just a ISR G2, depending on size of location.				
Authenticates remote users and branch sites.				
Incorporates the enterprise WAN links.				
Uses multicast traffic and QoS to optimize network traffic.				
Connects users with campus, server farm, and enterprise edge.				
Mobile users connect using a local ISP.				
High availability through resilient hierarchical network design.				
Converges voice, video, and data across a single IP communications network.				
Offsite data center to provide disaster recovery and business continuance services.				

Cisco Enterprise Architecture Feature	Enterprise Campus	Enterprise Edge	Service Provider Edge	Remote
Devices located here include firewall and firewall routers, and network intrusion prevention systems.				
Routes traffic into the Campus Core submodule.				
Access management with VLANs and IPsec.				
Supports security over Layer 2 and Layer 3 WANs.				
Provides internal users with secure connectivity to Internet services.				

In Figure 10-2, label the modules and submodules of the Cisco Enterprise Architecture model.

Figure 10-2   Cisco Enterprise Architecture Model

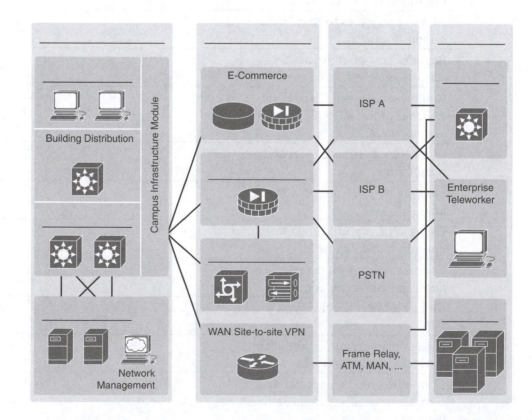

Evolving Network Architectures

Network architectures need to rapidly evolve to meet the needs of users. Traditionally, employees and students alike used devices provided by the organization. However, you more than likely currently use some type of mobile device to conduct some of your business or school work. Today's enterprise networks should seamlessly provide services to users of all modes of access.

Cisco Enterprise Architectures

What are the top trends that are impacting networks?

What network architectures has Cisco introduced to address these trends?

Emerging Network Architectures

What are the two primary sets of services provided by the Cisco Borderless Network Architecture?

What are the three layers of the Cisco Collaboration Architecture?

What are the three components of the Cisco Data Center/Virtualization Architecture?

In Table 10-6, indicate the emerging network architecture described by the feature or service.

Table 10-6   Emerging Network Architectures

Emerging Network Architecture Functions and Services	Cisco Borderless Networks	Cisco Collaboration Architecture	Cisco Data Center/ Virtualization Architecture
Comprehensive set of technologies that bring together the network, computing, and storage platforms.			
Applications include WebEx Meeting, WebEx Social, Cisco Jabber, and TelePresence.			
Any device must be able to connect securely, reliably, and seamlessly from anywhere.			
Portfolio of products, applications, and software development kits that provide a comprehensive solution to allow people to cooperate and contribute to the production of something.			
Unified approach to deliver application services to users in a highly distributed environment.			
Network infrastructure and services are united via Cisco unified system services options.			

Packet Tracer
☐ Challenge

Packet Tracer - Skills Integration Challenge - OSPF (CN 1.4.1.2)

Packet Tracer - Skills Integration Challenge - EIGRP (CN 1.4.1.3)

CHAPTER 11

Connecting to the WAN

Wide-area networks (WANs) are used to connect remote LANs together. Various technologies are used to achieve this connection. This chapter reviews WAN technologies and the many WAN services available.

WAN Technologies Overview

WAN access options differ in technology, speed, and price. Each has advantages and disadvantages. Selecting the best technology depends largely on the network design.

Network Types and Their Evolving WAN Needs

The WAN needs of a network depend greatly on the size of the network. These network types run the spectrum from small offices that really only need a broadband connection to the Internet all the way up to multinational enterprises that need a variety of WAN options to satisfy local, regional, and global restrictions.

In Table 11-1, indicate the network type that fits each of the descriptions. Some descriptions may apply to more than one network type.

Table 11-1   Identify the Network Type

Network Description	Small Office Network	Campus Network	Branch Network	Distributed Network
Outsourced IT support				
Very large-sized business				
Connectivity to the Internet				
Converged network and application services				
Hundreds of employees				
Home, branch, and regional offices, teleworkers, and a central office				
Limited number of employees				
In-house IT staff and network support				
Thousands of employees				
Several remote, branch, and regional offices (one central office)				
Small-sized business				
LAN focus of operations with broadband				
Small to medium-sized business				
Multiple campus LANs				
Medium-sized business				

WAN Operations and Terminology

WANs operate at which layers of the OSI model?

Which organizations are responsible for WAN standards?

What are some of the Layer 2 WAN technologies?

Why is the Layer 2 address field not usually used in WAN services?

Match the definition on the left with a term on the right. This exercise is a one-to-one matching.

Definitions

a. The boundary between customer equipment and service provider equipment

b. Devices inside the enterprise edge wiring closet that are owned or leased by the organization

c. Provider equipment that resides in the WAN backbone capable of supporting routing protocols

d. Digital modem used by DSL or cable Internet service providers

e. Dynamically establishes a dedicated circuit before communication starts

f. Provides an interface to connect subscribers to a WAN link

g. Splits traffic so that it can be routed over the shared network

h. Local service provider facility that connects the CPE to the provider network

i. Physical connection between the CPE to the CO

j. Required by digital leased lines to provide termination of the digital signal and convert into frames ready for transmission on the LAN

k. Consists of the all-digital, long-haul communications lines, switches, routers, and other equipment in the provider network

l. Customer device that provides internetworking and WAN access interface ports

m. Customer device that transmits data over the WAN link

n. Multiport device that sits at the service provider edge to switch traffic

o. Legacy technology device that converts digital signals into analog signals transmitted over telephone lines

p. Legacy technology device that can support hundreds of dial-in and dial-out users

Terms

_____ Packet-switched network

_____ WAN switch

_____ Customer premises equipment (CPE)

_____ Central office (CO)

_____ Dialup modem

_____ Access server

_____ Data communications equipment (DCE)

_____ Router

_____ Data terminal equipment (DTE)

_____ Local loop

_____ CSU/DSU

_____ Circuit-switched network

_____ Demarcation point

_____ Broadband modem

_____ Toll network

_____ Core multilayer switch

Selecting a WAN Technology

The WAN access connections your small to medium-sized business purchases could use a public or private WAN infrastructure—or a mix of both. Each type provides various WAN technologies. Understanding which WAN access connections and technologies are best suited to your situation is an important part of network design.

Varieties of WAN Link Connections

Your ISP can recommend several WAN link connection options that based on your specific requirements. These options can be classified in various categories. Use the list of WAN access options to label Figure 11-1.

Figure 11-1   WAN Access Options

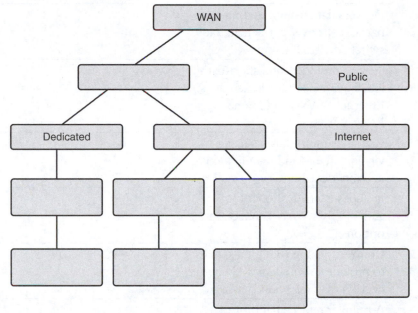

Labels

T1/E1/T3/E3	ATM	Switched
Frame Relay	Circuit switched	Packet switched
Metro Ethernet	Cable	Wireless
MPLS	PSTN	DSL
VPN	Private	Broadband
ISDN	Leased lines	

Private and Public WAN Access Options

As shown in Figure 11-1, WAN access options can first be classified as either private or public. Table 11-2 lists descriptions for various private WAN access options. Indicate which one is described. Some options are described more than once.

Table 11-2   Private WAN Access Options

Private WAN Access Options	Leased Lines	MPLS	Ethernet WAN	ATM	ISDN	VSAT	Dialup	Frame Relay
Considered the most expensive of all WAN access technologies.								
Analog telephone lines are used to provide a switched WAN connection.								
A permanent, dedicated WAN connection which uses a T- or E-carrier system.								
Satellite to router communications for WAN connections.								
Delivers data using fixed 53-byte packet cells over permanent and switched virtual circuits.								
Service providers and short-path labeling are used for leased lines, Ethernet WANs, and Frame Relay WANs.								
Connects multiple sites using virtual circuits and data-link connection identifiers.								
Includes MetroE, EoMPLS, and VPLS as WAN connection options.								
Converts analog to digital signals to provide a switched WAN connection over telephone lines.								
A popular replacement for traditional Frame Relay and ATM WAN access technologies.								

Match the definition on the left with a public WAN access option on the right. This exercise is a one-to-one matching.

Definitions

a. Radio and directional-antenna modem WAN access option provided to public organizations

b. WAN access option that uses telephone lines to transport data via multiplexed links

c. High-speed long-distance wireless connections through nearby special service provider towers

d. Cellular radio waves WAN access option used with smartphones and tablets

e. Dish and modem-based WAN access option for rural users where cable and DSL are not available

f. Secure Internet-based WAN access option used by teleworkers and extranet users

g. Entire networks connected together by using VPN routers, firewalls, and security appliances

h. A shared WAN access option that transports data using television-signal networks

Public WAN Access Options

_____ 3G/4G Cellular

_____ VPN Remote

_____ WiMax

_____ Satellite Internet

_____ DSL

_____ Cable

_____ Municipal WiFi

_____ VPN site-to-site

Lab - Researching WAN Technologies (CN 2.2.4.3)

CHAPTER 12

Point-to-Point Connections

Point-to-point connections are the most common type of WAN connections. These connections are also called serial or leased lines. This chapter reviews the terms, technology, and protocols used in serial connections.

Serial Point-to-Point Overview

Understanding how point-to-point serial communication across a leased line works is important to an overall understanding of how WANs function.

Serial Communications

Briefly explain the difference between serial and parallel communications.

What is clock skew issue in parallel communications?

Match the serial communications definition on the left with a term on the right. This is a one-to-one matching exercise.

Definitions

a. Cable that allows two WAN end devices to be directly connected together

b. Signals sent sequentially 1 bit after another

c. A networking device that converts signals into an ISP WAN circuit format

d. Universal ports that have replaced both RS-232 and parallel ports on newer PCs

e. A WAN connection that interconnects two LANs directly

f. The point at the customer site where the ISP network ends

g. A technique that reassembles multiple data transmissions

h. The OSI layer where time-division multiplexing (TDM) operates

i. A WAN technology that uses TDM

j. The way that STDM divides bandwidth into multiple slots for data transmission

k. Provides a clocking signal for the WAN circuit

l. LAN/WAN routers at the customer location

m. Transmission signals split between multiple wires concurrently

n. The network equipment connected to the WAN circuit at the customer location

Terms

_____ Physical

_____ DCE

_____ Demarc

_____ CPE

_____ ISDN

_____ DTE

_____ Variable

_____ Parallel

_____ CSU/DSU

_____ USB

_____ Leased line

_____ Null modem

_____ Serial

_____ Bit interleaving

WAN Protocols

Just like LANs, data is encapsulated into frames before transmission onto a WAN link. Various encapsulation protocols can be used to achieve the framing. In Table 12-1, indicate which protocol best fits the description.

Table 12-1   WAN Encapsulation Protocols

WAN Protocol Description	HDLC	PPP	SLIP	X.25/LAPB	Frame Relay	ATM
Provides connections over synchronous and asynchronous circuits						
International standard for cell relay						
Predecessor to Frame Relay						
Default encapsulation on a serial link between two Cisco devices						
Eliminates the need for error correction and flow control						
Forms the basis for synchronous PPP						
Built-in security with PAP and CHAP						
Transfers data 53 bytes at a time so that processing can occur in hardware						
Next-generation protocol after X.25						
Largely replaced by PPP						
An ITU-T standard that defines connections between a DTE and DCE						

HDLC Encapsulation

What is the major difference between the ISO 13239 HDLC standard and Cisco's implementation of HDLC?

In Figure 12-1, label the fields of Cisco HDLC frame.

Figure 12-1   Cisco HDLC Frame Format

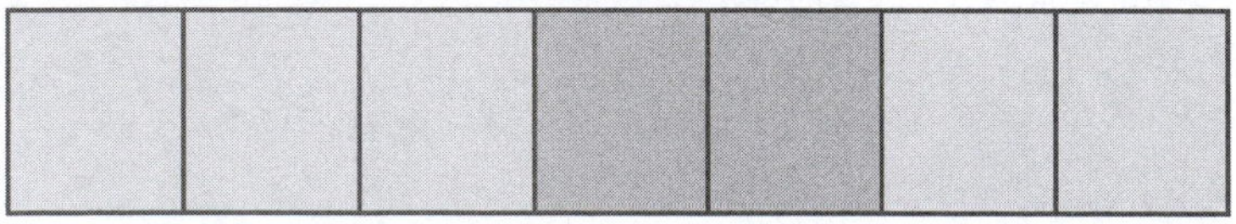

List the three different formats of the Control field.

_____

_____

_____

HDLC Configuration and Troubleshooting

Although High-Level Data Link Control (HDLC) is the default encapsulation on Cisco synchronous serial lines, you may need to change the encapsulation back to HDLC. Record the commands, including the router prompt, to change the first serial interface on a 1900 series router to HDLC.

Troubleshooting Serial Interfaces

Troubleshooting the cause of a serial interface issue usually begins by entering the **show interface serial** command. This command can return one of six possible statuses for the line. In Table 12-2, indicate what status would display for each of the conditions of the serial interface. Some statuses are used more than once.

Table 12-2   Line Conditions and Status Indicators

Condition of the Serial Interface	Serial X Is Up, Line Protocol Is Up	Serial X Is Down, Line Protocol Is Down	Serial X Is Up, Line Protocol Is Down	Serial X Is Up, Line Protocol Is Up (Looped)	Serial X Is Up, Line Protocol Is Down (Disabled)	Serial X Is Administratively Down, Line Protocol Is Down
A high error rate has occurred due to a WAN service provider problem.						
Keepalives are not being sent by the remote router.						
The router configuration includes the **shutdown** interface configuration command.						
Cabling is faulty or incorrect.						
The **clockrate** command is not configured on the interface.						
This is the proper status line condition.						
The router is not sensing a carrier detect (CD) signal.						
The same random sequence number in the keepalive is returned over the link.						

What command will show whether a DTE or DCE cable is attached to the interface?

Packet Tracer
☐ Activity

Packet Tracer - Troubleshooting Serial Interfaces (CN 3.1.2.7)

PPP Operation

PPP encapsulation has been carefully designed to retain compatibility with most commonly used supporting hardware. PPP encapsulates data frames for transmission over Layer 2 physical links.

PPP Components

Briefly described the three main components of PPP.

-
-
-

In Figure 12-2, fill in the missing parts of the PPP layered architecture.

Figure 12-2   PPP Layered Architecture

List the type of physical interfaces supported by PPP.

-
-
-
-

What automatic configurations does the Link Control Protocol (LCP) provide at each end of the link?

- ■

- ■

- ■

- ■

Briefly describe how PPP uses Network Control Protocol (NCP).

In Table 12-3, indicate whether each characteristic describes LCP or NCP.

Table 12-3   LCP and NCP Characteristics

Characteristic	LCP	NCP
Can configure authentication, compression, and error detection		
Bring network layer protocols up and down		
Encapsulate and negotiate options for IPv4 and IPv6		
Negotiate and set up control options on the WAN circuit		
Handles limits on packet size		
Establish, configure, and test the data link connection		
Uses standardized codes to indicate the network layer protocol		
Determine if link is functioning properly		
Terminate the link		
Manage packets from several network layer protocols		

Figure 12-3 shows the PPP frame format. Answer the following questions about the specific features and purpose of each field.

Figure 12-3   PPP Frame Format

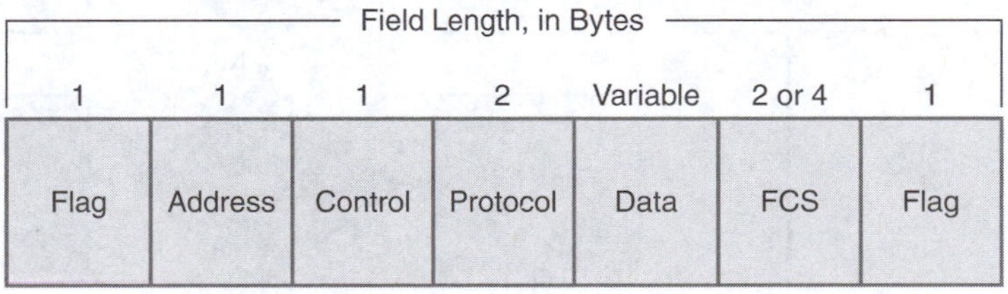

Field Length, in Bytes						
1	1	1	2	Variable	2 or 4	1
Flag	Address	Control	Protocol	Data	FCS	Flag

What is the bit pattern for the Flag field?

Why is the Address field all 1s or 0xFF?

What is the purpose of the Control field?

What is the purpose of the Protocol field?

What is the default size of the information stored in the Data field?

What does FCS stand for and what is the purpose of this field?

PPP Sessions

What are the three phase for establishing a PPP session?

-
-
-

Figure 12-4 shows a partially labeled flowchart for the LCP link negotiation process. Complete the flowchart by properly labeling it with the provided steps.

Figure 12-4   Steps in the LCP Link Negotiation Process

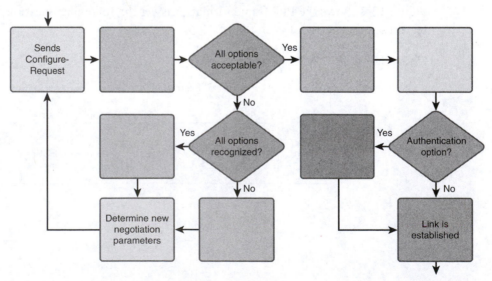

Missing Labels for Figure 12-4

- Send Configure-Reject

- Receive Configure-Ack

- Process Configure-Request

- Send Configure-Ack

- Authentication Phase

- Send Configure-Nak

PPP can be configured to support optional functions, including the following:

- _____ using either PAP or CHAP

- _____ using either Stacker or Predictor

- _____ that combines two or more channels to increase the WAN bandwidth

After the link is established, the LCP passes control to the appropriate NCP. Figure 12-5 shows the NCP process for IPv4. Complete the figure by properly labeling it with the provided phases and steps.

Missing Labels for Figure 12-5

- IPv4 Data Transfer

- NCP Termination

- IPCP Configure-Request

- IPCP Configure-Ack

- IPCP Terminate-Request

- LCP Maintenance

- IPCP Terminate-Ack

- NCP Configuration

Figure 12-5   The NCP Process

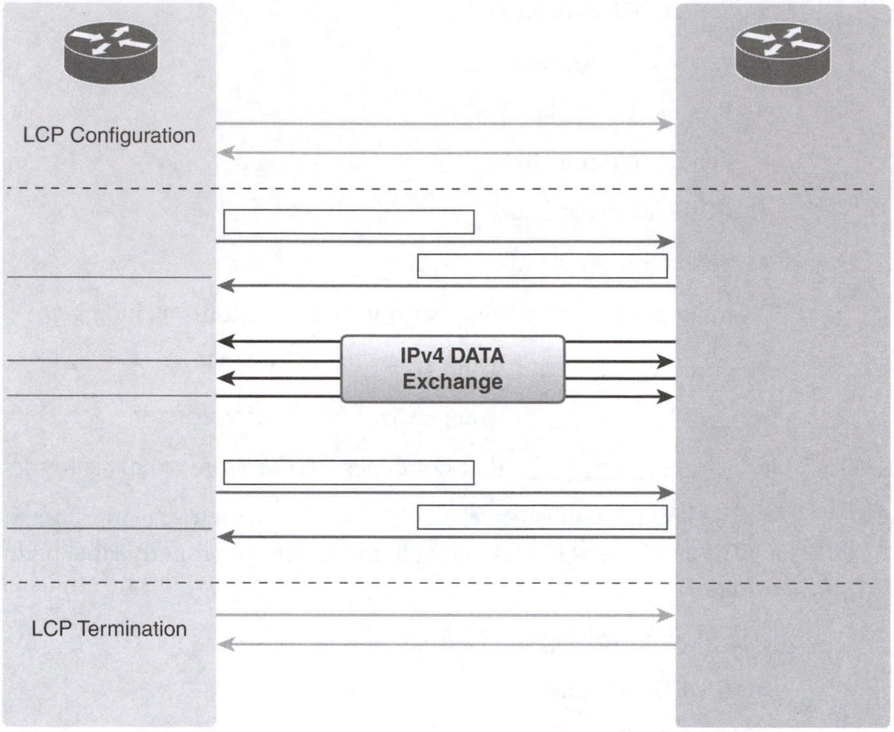

Configure PPP

PPP is a robust WAN protocol supporting multiple physical layer and network layer implementations. In addition, PPP has many optional features the network administrator can choose to implement.

Basic PPP Configuration with Options

Figure 12-6 shows the topology and Table 12-4 shows the addressing we will use for PPP configuration.

Figure 12-6   PPP Topology

Table 12-4   Addressing Table for PPP

Device	Interface	IPv4 Address	Subnet Mask
		IPv6 Address/Prefix	
RTA	S0/0/0	172.16.1.1	255.255.255.252
		2001:DB8:1:F::1/64	
RTB	S0/0/0	172.16.1.2	255.255.255.252
		2001:DB8:1:F::2/64	

Assume that the router interfaces are already configured with IPv4 and IPv6 addressing. RTB is fully configured with PPP. Record the commands, including the router prompt, to configure RTA with a basic PPP configuration.

RTB is configured for software compression using the Stacker compression algorithm. What happens if RTA is not configured with compression?

Record the command, including the router prompt, to configure the same compression on RTA.

RTB is configured to take down the link if the quality falls below 70 percent. Record the command, including the router prompt, to configure the equivalent on RTA.

In Figure 12-7, RTA and RTB are now using two serial links to transfer data. RTB is already configured with PPP multilink to load balance the traffic to RTA. Record the commands, including the router prompt, to configure the RTA multilink interface including IPv4 and IPv6 addressing and the necessary commands for the serial interfaces. Use the addressing in Table 12-4 for the multilink interface rather than Serial 0/0/0.

Figure 12-7   PPP Multilink Topology

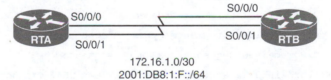

S0/0/0

S0/0/0

RTA   S0/0/1

S0/0/1   RTB

172.16.1.0/30
2001:DB8:1:F::/64

You can verify the operation of PPP using the following **show** commands. Record the commands used to generate the output on RTA.

```
RTA# _____
Serial0/0/0 is up, line protocol is up
  Hardware is WIC MBRD Serial
  Internet address is 172.16.1.1/30
  MTU 1500 bytes, BW 1544 Kbit/sec, DLY 20000 usec,
     reliability 255/255, txload 1/255, rxload 1/255
  Encapsulation PPP, LCP Open
   Open: IPCP, IPV6CP, CCP, CDPCP, loopback not set
  Keepalive set (10 sec)
<output omitted>


RTA# _____


Multilink1
  Bundle name: RTA
  Remote Endpoint Discriminator: [1] RTB
  Local Endpoint Discriminator: [1] RTA
  Bundle up for 00:01:20, total bandwidth 3088, load 1/255
  Receive buffer limit 24000 bytes, frag timeout 1000 ms
    0/0 fragments/bytes in reassembly list
    0 lost fragments, 0 reordered
    0/0 discarded fragments/bytes, 0 lost received
    0x2 received sequence, 0x2 sent sequence
  Member links: 2 active, 0 inactive (max 255, min not set)
    Se0/0/0, since 00:01:20
    Se0/0/1, since 00:01:06
No inactive multilink interfaces
```

PPP Authentication

Briefly explain the difference between PAP and CHAP.

PAP is not interactive. When you configure an interface with the _____ command, the username and password are sent as one LCP data package. You are not prompted for a username. The receiving node checks the username and password combination and either accepts or rejects the connection.

List three situations where PAP would be the appropriate choice for authentication.

- ▪
- ▪
- ▪

Once PAP authentication is established, the link is vulnerable to attack. Why?

CHAP challenges periodically to make sure that the remote node still has a valid password. Complete the missing information in the following steps as RTA authenticates with RTB using CHAP.

Step 1.   RTA initially negotiates the link connection using LCP with router RTB, and the two systems agree to use CHAP authentication during the PPP LCP negotiation.

Step 2.   RTB generates an _____ and a _____ number, and sends that and its _____ as a CHAP challenge packet to RTA.

Step 3.   RTA uses the _____ of the challenger (RTB) and cross references it with its local database to find its associated _____. RTA then generates a unique _____ number using the RTB's _____, _____, _____ number, and the shared _____.

Step 4.   RTA then sends the challenge _____, the _____ value, and its _____ (RTA) to RTB.

Step 5.   RTB generates its own _____ value using the _____, the shared _____, and the _____ number it originally sent to RTA.

Step 6.   RTB compares its _____ value with the _____ value sent by RTA. If the values are the same, RTB sends a link established response to RTA.

When authentication is local (no AAA/TACACS+), what is the command syntax to configure PPP authentication on an interface?

Assume that both PAP and CHAP are configured with the command **ppp authentication chap pap** on the interface. Explain how authentication will proceed.

PAP Configuration

In Figure 12-6, RTB is already configured with PAP authentication with the password cisco123. Record the commands to configure PAP on RTA.

CHAP Configuration

CHAP uses one less command than PAP. Now record the commands to remove PAP and configure RTA to use CHAP authentication.

Packet Tracer - Configuring PAP and CHAP Authentication (CN 3.3.2.7)

Lab - Configuring Basic PPP with Authentication (CN 3.3.2.8)

Troubleshoot WAN Connectivity

If you cannot ping across a PPP link and you have checked the physical and data link layer issues reviewed in the "Troubleshooting Serial Interfaces" section earlier, the issue is probably the PPP configuration. You can use the **debug** command to troubleshoot PPP issues using the **debug ppp** {*parameter*} syntax. Based on the descriptions in Table 12-5, fill in the corresponding parameter you would use with the **debug ppp** command.

Table 12-5   Parameters for the debug ppp Command

Parameter	Usage
	Displays issues associated with PPP connection negotiation and operation
	Displays information specific to the exchange of PPP connections using MPPC
	Displays PPP packets transmitted during PPP startup
	Displays PPP packets being sent and received
	Displays authentication protocol messages
	Displays protocol errors and statistics associated with PPP connection negotiations using MSCB

Lab - Troubleshooting Basic PPP with Authentication (CN 3.4.1.5)

Packet Tracer
☐ Activity

Packet Tracer - Troubleshooting PPP with Authentication (CN 3.4.1.4)

Packet Tracer - Skills Integration Challenge (CN 3.5.1.2)

CHAPTER 13

Frame Relay

Although newer services are rapidly replacing it in some locations, Frame Relay has been a popular alternative to expensive dedicated leased lines. Frame Relay provides a cost-efficient solution for WAN access between multiple sites. This chapter reviews Frame Relay technology, configuration, verification, and troubleshooting.

Introduction to Frame Relay

Frame Relay is a high-performance WAN protocol that operates at the physical and data link layers of the OSI reference model. Unlike leased lines, Frame Relay requires only a single access circuit to the Frame Relay provider to communicate with other sites connected to the same provider.

Frame Relay Concepts and Terminology

Match the definition on the left with a term on the right. Terms are only used once.

Definitions

a. Bandwidth "borrowing" from other PVCs when available

b. Read Frame Relay was popular when compared to private leased lines

c. A preconfigured logical path between two endpoints and assigned a DLCI

d. A logical connection that is established dynamically for the time needed

e. The equivalent of 24 DS0 channels

f. Guaranteed bandwidth for a specific PVC

g. Downstream notification that there is congestion on a Frame Relay switch

h. Manual configuration will do this to the auto-sensing of LMI-type feature on Cisco routers

i. Holding frame in a buffer before sending

j. Frame Relay extension that allows the DTE to discover the list of available DLCIs configured on the access link

k. A PVC that no longer exists

l. Used to identify each Frame Relay circuit endpoint

m. Port bandwidth of the local loop

n. One of the three LMI types other than cisco and q933a

o. LMI provides these updates about Frame Relay connectivity

p. Identifies the frames to be dropped in times of congestion

q. Process used by LMI to associate network layer addresses to data link layer addresses

r. The end of the Frame Relay connection that initiates requests about the status of its Frame Relay links

s. Protocol replaced by Frame Relay

Terms

_____ Access rate

_____ ANSI

_____ Black hole

_____ Bursting

_____ CIR

_____ Cost savings

_____ DE

_____ Disable

_____ DLCI

_____ DTE

_____ FECN

_____ Inverse ARP

_____ LMI

_____ PVC

_____ Queuing

_____ Status

_____ SVC

_____ T1

_____ X.25

Frame Relay Operation

Frame Relay networks use _____ (_____), which uniquely define a logical path between two endpoints. Frame Relay is a more cost-effective option than leased lines for two reasons:

The end of each _____ uses a number to identify it called the _____ (_____). What does it mean to say that these numbers are locally significant?

Frame Relay is _____, meaning that it transmits only one frame at a time, but that many logical connections can coexist on a single physical line.

In Figure 13-1, label the missing fields in a standard Frame Relay frame.

Figure 13-1   Fields of the Standard Frame Relay Frame

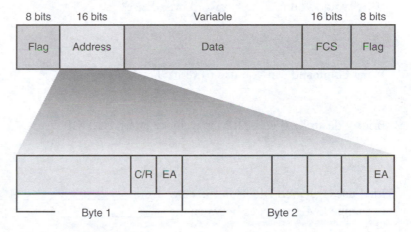

Identify and briefly describe each of the three Frame Relay topologies.

A router must know what remote Layer 3 address maps to the locally configured DLCI before it can send data over the link. This mapping can be achieved statically or dynamically.

Briefly describe the IPv4 protocol that provides dynamic mapping.

On Cisco routers, what must you do to make sure Inverse ARP is operational?

What is the command syntax to disable Inverse ARP?

What is the command syntax to override dynamic mapping and statically configure the map?

Why would you use the keyword **ietf**?

Why would you use the keyword **broadcast**?

What command can you use to verify Frame Relay maps?

Briefly describe the Local Management Interface (LMI).

LMI uses reserved DLCIs in the range from _____ to _____ to exchange LMI messages between the _____ and _____.

What are the three LMI types supported by Cisco routers?

With Cisco IOS software release 11.2, the LMI type does not need to be configured because it is _____.

In Figure 13-2, RTA and RTB are both configured to use Frame Relay with the IPv4 addressing and DLCIs shown. RTA has just booted up. Fully explain how RTA will dynamically learn the DLCIs from the local Frame Relay switch and then dynamically learn the IPv4 address of RTB.

Figure 13-2   Frame Relay Topology

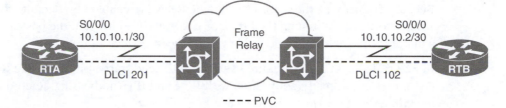

From the customer's point of view, Frame Relay is one interface configured with one or more PVCs. The rate at which data will be accepted by the local Frame Relay switch is contracted. The _____ is the actual speed of the port connected to the service provider. It is not possible to send data any faster. The _____ (_____) is the rate at which the customer can send data into the Frame Relay network. All data at or below this rate is guaranteed.

What does the term oversubscription mean in relation to Frame Relay? What problems can it cause?

When the Frame Relay network is underutilized, customers can _____ over their CIR at no additional cost. The _____ (_____) is a negotiated rate above the CIR that the customer can use to transmit for short bursts, and represents the maximum allowed traffic under normal working conditions. When sending at a rate higher than the CIR, the _____ (_____) bit is set to 1 in every frame so that the Frame Relay network can discard the frame if congestion is occurring.

However, when there is congestion on the Frame Relay network, the switch that is experiencing congestion will begin setting the _____ (_____) bit to _____ to inform downstream devices that there is congestion on the network. It will also set the _____ (_____) bit to _____and send a message to the source to throttle back the speed at which it is sending data. In addition, the Frame Relay switch experiencing congestion will _____ every frame that has the DE bit set to 1.

Configure Frame Relay

Frame Relay connections are created by configuring customer premise equipment (CPE) routers or other devices to communicate with a service provider Frame Relay switch. The service provider configures the Frame Relay switch, which helps keep end-user configuration tasks to a minimum.

Configure Basic Frame Relay

Because so many of the features of Frame Relay are enabled by default, configuration is straightforward. Assuming the interface is correctly addressed, the basic configuration is simply a matter of changing the encapsulation on the interface.

In Figure 13-3, RTB is configured and ready to send traffic on the Frame Relay network. Assume RTA is already configured with IPv4 and IPv6 addressing. Record the commands, including the router prompt, to enable Frame Relay.

Figure 13-3

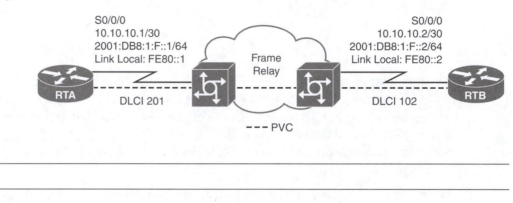

Connectivity between RTA and RTB should now be operational for IPv4 traffic. However, in our example, IPv6 requires static mapping. You will need to map both the globally unique and link local IPv6 addresses. Because the link local address is used for multicasts, you will need to add the keyword _____ to your frame relay map configuration. Record the commands, including the router prompt, to statically configure RTA with IPv6 frame relay maps.

Record the command used to generate the following output verifying the IPv4 and IPv6 maps.

```
RTA# _____
Serial0/0/0 (up): ipv6 FE80::2 dlci 201(0xC9,0x3090), static,
          broadcast,
          CISCO, status defined, active
Serial0/0/0 (up): ipv6 2001:DB8:1:F::2 dlci 201(0xC9,0x3090), static,
          CISCO, status defined, active
Serial0/0/0 (up): ip 10.10.10.2 dlci 201(0xC9,0x3090), dynamic,
          broadcast,
          CISCO, status defined, active
```

Packet Tracer - Configuring Static Frame Relay Maps (CN 4.2.1.4)

Packet Tracer
☐ Activity

Configure Subinterfaces

When configuring a hub-and-spoke topology with Frame Relay, you must create subinterfaces so that each PVC can have its own Layer 3 addressing. In a Frame Relay nonbroadcast multi-access (NBMA) topology like the one shown in Figure 13-4, this can cause reachability issues without proper configuration.

Figure 13-4   Frame Relay NBMA Topology

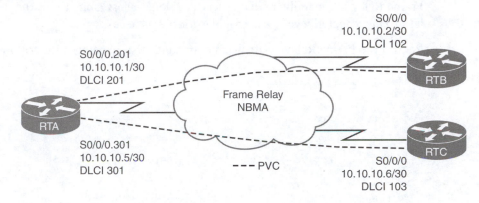

Briefly describe the three reachability issues caused by NBMA topologies.

What are the three ways to solve these reachability issues?

In Figure 13-4, RTA is the hub router and RTB and RTC are spokes. Given the information shown in Figure 13-4, record the commands, including the router prompts, to configure RTA with Frame Relay using point-to-point subinterfaces.

Packet Tracer
☐ **Activity**

Lab - Configuring Frame Relay and Subinterfaces (CN 4.2.2.7)

Packet Tracer - Configuring Frame Relay Point-to-Point Subinterfaces (CN 4.2.2.6)

Troubleshoot Connectivity

Frame Relay is generally a reliable service. Nonetheless, sometimes the network performs at less-than-expected levels, and troubleshooting is necessary.

Record the Frame Relay verification commands that generated the following output:

```
RTA# _____


PVC Statistics for interface Serial0/0/0 (Frame Relay DTE)


              Active      Inactive      Deleted      Static
  Local         1            0             0            0

  Switched      0            0             0            0

  Unused        0            0             0            0


DLCI = 201, DLCI USAGE = LOCAL, PVC STATUS = ACTIVE, INTERFACE = Serial0/0/0


  input pkts 1          output pkts 1          in bytes 34
  out bytes 34          dropped pkts 0         in pkts dropped 0
  out pkts dropped 0            out bytes dropped 0
  in FECN pkts 0        in BECN pkts 0         out FECN pkts 0
  out BECN pkts 0       in DE pkts 0           out DE pkts 0
  out bcast pkts 1      out bcast bytes 34
  5 minute input rate 0 bits/sec, 0 packets/sec
  5 minute output rate 0 bits/sec, 0 packets/sec
  pvc create time 00:02:12, last time pvc status changed 00:01:38
RTA# _____


LMI Statistics for interface Serial0/0/0 (Frame Relay DTE) LMI TYPE = CISCO
  Invalid Unnumbered info 0        Invalid Prot Disc 0
  Invalid dummy Call Ref 0         Invalid Msg Type 0
  Invalid Status Message 0         Invalid Lock Shift 0
  Invalid Information ID 0         Invalid Report IE Len 0
  Invalid Report Request 0         Invalid Keep IE Len 0
  Num Status Enq. Sent 14          Num Status msgs Rcvd 15
  Num Update Status Rcvd 0         Num Status Timeouts 0
  Last Full Status Req 00:00:23    Last Full Status Rcvd 00:00:23
```

```
RTA# _____

Serial0/0/0 is up, line protocol is up

  Hardware is WIC MBRD Serial

  Internet address is 10.10.10.1/30

  MTU 1500 bytes, BW 1544 Kbit/sec, DLY 20000 usec,

      reliability 255/255, txload 1/255, rxload 1/255

  Encapsulation FRAME-RELAY, loopback not set

  Keepalive set (10 sec)

  LMI enq sent  15, LMI stat recvd 16, LMI upd recvd 0, DTE LMI up

  LMI enq recvd 0, LMI stat sent  0, LMI upd sent  0

  LMI DLCI 1023  LMI type is CISCO  frame relay DTE

  FR SVC disabled, LAPF state down

  Broadcast queue 0/64, broadcasts sent/dropped 1/0, interface

  <output omitted>


RTA# _____

Serial0/0/0 (up): ip 10.10.10.2 dlci 201(0xC9,0x3090), dynamic,

            broadcast,

            CISCO, status defined, active

Serial0/0/0 (up): ipv6 2001:DB8:1:F::2 dlci 201(0xC9,0x3090), static,

            CISCO, status defined, active

Serial0/0/0 (up): ipv6 FE80::2 dlci 201(0xC9,0x3090), static,

            broadcast,

            CISCO, status defined, active

RTA#
```

In Table 13-1, indicate which command enables you to verify the described information. Some information can be verified with more than one command.

Table 13-1   Frame Relay Verification Commands

Frame Relay Information Verified	show interface serial	show frame-relay lmi	show frame-relay pvc	show frame-relay map
Broadcast status for the PVC				
PVC status				
Number of LMI status queries sent and received				
Layer 1 and Layer 2 status information				
LMI type				
Invalid LMI types				
Number of ECN packets in and out				

Frame Relay Information Verified	show interface serial	show frame-relay lmi	show frame-relay pvc	show frame-relay map
DLCI assigned to the PVC				
The encapsulation type				
Frame Relay DTE/DCE type				

Packet Tracer
☐ Challenge

Packet Tracer - Skills Integration Challenge (CN 4.4.1.2)

CHAPTER 14

Network Address Translation for IPv4

All public IPv4 addresses that transverse the Internet must be registered with a Regional Internet Registry (RIR). Only the registered holder of a public Internet address can assign that address to a network device. With the proliferation of personal computing and the advent of the World Wide Web, it soon became obvious that 4.3 billion IPv4 addresses would not be enough. The long-term solution was to eventually be IPv6. But for the short term, several solutions were implemented by the IETF, including Network Address Translation (NAT) and RFC 1918 private IPv4 addresses.

NAT Operation

There are not enough public IPv4 addresses to assign a unique address to each device connected to the Internet. Networks are commonly implemented using private IPv4 addresses.

NAT Characteristics

Fill in the table with the private addresses defined by RFC 1918.

Class	Address Range	CIDR Prefix
A		
B		
C		

Briefly explain the following terms:

- Inside local address:

- Inside global address:

- Outside global address:

- Outside local address:

In Figure 14-1, label each type of NAT address.

Figure 14-1   Identify NAT Address Types

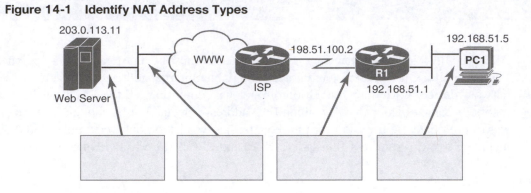

Types and Benefits of NAT

Briefly describe the three types of NAT:

- Static address translation (static NAT):

- Dynamic address translation (dynamic NAT):

- Port Address Translation (PAT):

When is it appropriate to use static NAT?

What is the difference between dynamic NAT and PAT?

List and explain at least three advantages and three disadvantages to using NAT.

Advantages

-
-
-
-

Disadvantages

■

■

■

■

■

**Packet Tracer
☐ Activity**

Packet Tracer - Investigating NAT Operation (RSE 11.1.2.6/WAN 5.1.2.6)

Configuring NAT

Configuring NAT is straightforward if you follow a few simple steps. Static NAT and dynamic NAT configurations vary slightly. Adding PAT to a dynamic NAT is as simple as adding a keyword to the configuration.

Configuring Static NAT

Use the following steps to configure static NAT:

Step 1. Create a map between the inside local IP address and the inside global IP address with the **ip nat inside source static local-ip global-ip** global configuration command.

Step 2. Configure the inside interface of the LAN the device is attached to participate in NAT with the **ip nat inside** interface configuration command.

Step 3. Configure the outside interface where NAT translation will occur with the **ip nat outside** interface configuration command.

Refer to the topology in Figure 14-2 to configure static NAT.

Figure 14-2   Static NAT Configuration Topology

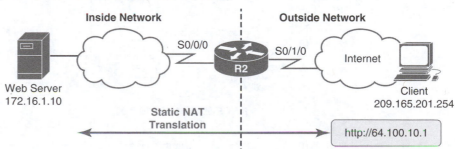

The web server uses an inside local address 172.16.1.10 that needs to be translated to the inside global address 64.100.10.1. Record the command including router prompt to configure the static translation on R2.

Record the commands including router prompt to configure the inside interface.

Record the commands including router prompt to configure the outside interface.

Packet Tracer - Configuring Static NAT (RP 11.2.1.4/WAN 5.2.1.4)

Configuring Dynamic NAT

Use the following steps to configure dynamic NAT:

Step 1.   Define the pool of addresses that will be used for dynamic translation using the **ip nat pool** *name start-ip end-ip* {**netmask** *netmask* | **prefix-length** *prefix-length*} global configuration command.

Step 2.   Configure an ACL to specify which inside local addresses will be translated using a standard ACL.

Step 3.   Bind the NAT pool to the ACL with the **ip nat inside source list** *ACL-number* **pool** *name* global configuration command.

Step 4.   Configure the inside interface of the LAN the device is attached to participate in NAT with the **ip nat inside** interface configuration command.

Step 5.   Configure the outside interface where NAT translation will occur with the **ip nat outside** interface configuration command.

Refer to the topology in Figure 14-3 to configure dynamic NAT.

Figure 14-3   Dynamic NAT Configuration Topology

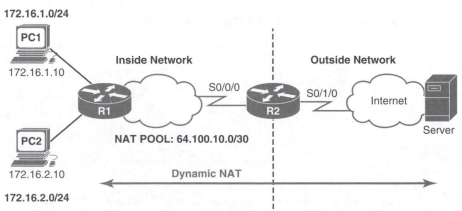

The pool of available addresses is 64.100.10.0/30. Record the command including router prompt to configure the NAT pool with an appropriate name.

The two LANs, 172.16.1.0/24 and 172.16.2.0/24, need to be translated. No other addresses are allowed. Record the command including router prompt to configure the ACL.

Record the command including router prompt to bind the NAT pool to the ACL.

Record the commands including router prompt to configure the inside interface.

Record the commands including router prompt to configure the outside interface.

Lab - Configuring Dynamic and Static NAT (RP 11.2.2.6/WAN 5.2.2.6)

Packet Tracer - Configuring Dynamic NAT (RP 11.2.2.5/WAN 5.2.2.5)

Packet Tracer
☐ Activity

Configuring Port Address Translation

Configuring Port Address Translation (PAT) is just like configuring dynamic NAT except you add the keyword **overload** to your binding configuration:

```
Router(config)# ip nat inside source list ACL-number pool name overload
```

However, a more common solution in a small business enterprise network is to simply overload the IP address on the gateway router. In fact, this is what a home router does "out of the box."

To configure NAT to overload the public IP address on an interface, use the following command:

```
Router(config)# ip nat inside source list ACL-number interface type number overload
```

In this case, of course, there is no pool configuration.

Refer to the topology in Figure 14-4 to configure PAT.

Figure 14-4   Dynamic NAT Configuration Topology

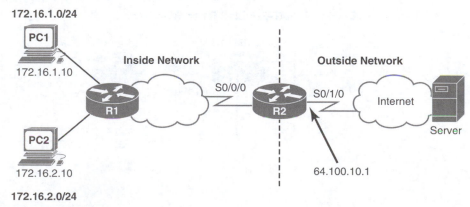

R1 is using the public IP address 64.100.10.1 on the Serial 0/1/0 interface. Record the command including router prompt to bind the ACL you configured for dynamic NAT to the Serial 0/1/0 interface.

_____

That's it! The rest of the commands are the same as dynamic NAT. However, the process of translating inbound and outbound packets is a bit more involved. PAT maintains a table of inside and outside addresses mapped to port numbers to track connections between the source and destination.

The series of Figures 14-5 through 14-8 illustrate the PAT process overloading an interface address. Use the options in Table 14-1 to fill in the source address (SA), destination address (DA), and corresponding port numbers as the packet travels from source to destination and back.

Table 14-1   Addresses and Port Numbers

64.100.10.2	192.168.51.5	1268	209.165.201.11
1150	53	192.168.51.1	80

Figure 14-5   Hop 1: PC1 to NAT-Enabled R1

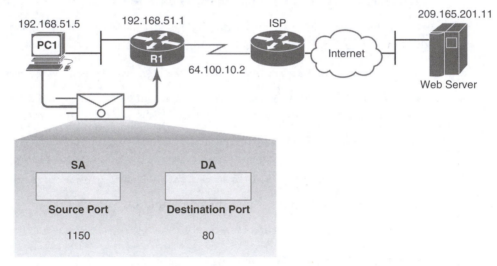

Figure 14-6   Hop 2: NAT-Enabled R1 to Web Server

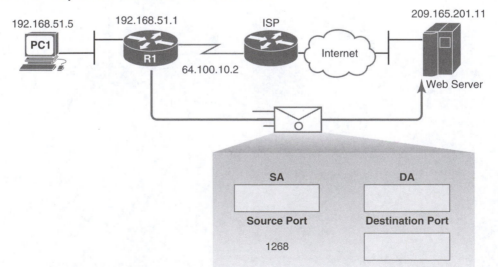

Figure 14-7   Hop 3: Web Server to NAT-Enable R1

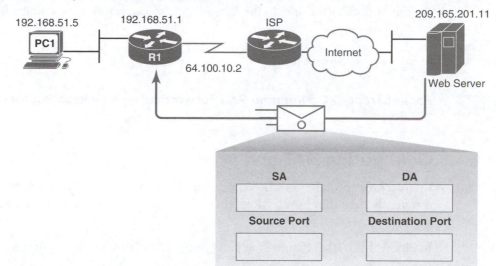

Figure 14-8   Hop 4: NAT-Enabled R1 to PC1

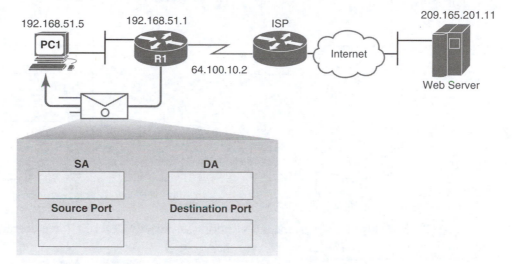

Lab - Configuring NAT Pool Overload and PAT (RP 11.2.3.7/WAN 5.2.3.7)

Packet Tracer - Implementing Static and Dynamic NAT (RP 11.2.3.6/WAN 5.2.3.6)

A Word About Port Forwarding

Because NAT hides internal addresses, peer-to-peer connections work only from the inside out, where NAT can map outgoing requests against incoming replies. The problem is that NAT does not allow requests initiated from the outside. To resolve this problem, you can configure port forwarding to identify specific ports that can be forwarded to inside hosts.

The port forwarding configuration is commonly done in a GUI. However, you can also configure port forwarding in the Cisco IOS adding the following command to your NAT configuration:

```
Router(config)# ip nat inside source {static {tcp | udp local-ip local-port global-ip global-port} [extendable]
```

Packet Tracer
☐ Activity

Packet Tracer - Configuring Port Forwarding on a Linksys Router (RP 11.2.4.4/WAN 5.2.4.4)

Configuring NAT and IPv6

IPv6 includes both its own IPv6 private address space and NAT, which are implemented differently than they are for IPv4. IPv6 uses a unique local address (ULA) for communication within a local site.

In Figure 14-9, label the missing parts of the IPv6 ULA address structure.

Figure 14-9   IPv6 Unique Local Address Structure

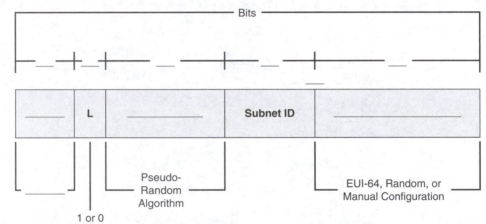

ULAs are also known as local IPv6 addresses. Briefly describe three characteristics of ULAs.

■

■

■

What is the main purpose of NAT for IPv6?

Briefly describe the three transition strategies to move from IPv4 to IPv6.

Troubleshooting NAT

When there are IPv4 connectivity problems in a NAT environment, it is often difficult to determine the cause of the problem. The first step in solving the problem is to rule out NAT as the cause. Follow these steps to verify that NAT is operating as expected:

Step 1. Review the purpose of the NAT configuration. Is there a static NAT implementation? Are the addresses in the dynamic pool actually valid? Are the inside and outside interfaces correctly identified?

Step 2. Verify that correct translations exist in the translation table using the **show ip nat translations** command.

Step 3. Use the **clear ip nat translations** * and **debug ip nat** commands to verify that NAT is operating as expected. Check to see whether dynamic entries are re-created after they are cleared.

Step 4. Review in detail what is happening to the packet, and verify that routers have the correct routing information to move the packet.

Lab - Troubleshooting NAT Configurations (RP 11.3.1.5/WAN 5.3.1.5)

Packet Tracer
☐ Activity

Packet Tracer - Verifying and Troubleshooting NAT Configurations (RP 11.3.1.4/WAN 5.3.1.4)

Packet Tracer - Skills Integration Challenge (RP 11.4.1.2/WAN 5.4.1.2)

CHAPTER 15

Broadband Solutions

With the advent of broadband technologies like digital subscriber line (DSL) and cable, working from home has become a popular option for both employees and companies alike. Virtual private networks (VPN) allow workers to securely connect to the business from remote locations. There are several factors to consider when choosing a broadband solution. This chapter reviews DLS, cable, wireless, VPN, and the factors to consider when implementing broadband solutions.

Teleworking

Teleworking is working away from the traditional workplace by using telecommunication technologies such as broadband and VPN security.

Benefits of Teleworking

The groups that benefit from teleworking include employees, employers, local governments, and communities. In Table 15-1, indicate which group primarily receives the benefit described.

Table 15-1   Benefits of Teleworking

Benefit	Employer	Government/Community	Individual
Improves employee morale			
Decreases recruitment and retention costs			
Reduces local infrastructure costs			
Attracts local employment and development			
Saving time or earning more in the same time			
Increases available time to care for dependents			
Reduces absenteeism levels			
Reduces the impact of urban drift			
Reduces costs associated with commuting			
Can reduce regional traffic delays			
Flexibility to deal with personal tasks			
Customers experience improved response times			

Costs of Teleworking

Teleworking does have some costs, as well. List at least two costs from the employer's perspective and two costs from the employee's perspective.

Employer

Employees

Business Requirements for Teleworker Services

Both the teleworker and the business must meet certain minimum requirements to implement teleworking services for the organization. In Table 15-2, indicate whether the teleworker or the company is responsible for each requirement.

Table 15-2   Teleworker Services Requirements

Responsibility	Teleworker	Company
Usually uses cable or DSL to access the VPN.		
Manages VPN authentication procedures.		
Uses client software for network access.		
Determines link aggregation and VPN termination methods.		
Uses network access while traveling.		
Maintains VPN concentrators and security appliances.		

Comparing Broadband Solutions

Depending on the location of the teleworker, connecting to the corporate network can be done in one of three ways: cable, DSL, or broadband wireless.

Cable

Cable broadband uses a coaxial cable that carries _____ (_____) signals across the network. What portion of the electromagnetic spectrum do these signals occupy?

Traditionally, cable communications was one way. Modern cable systems now provide two-way communication. What three main telecommunication services are offered by today's cable companies?

Two-way communications occurs _____ in the 50- to 860-MHz range and _____ in the 5- to 42-MHz range.

The _____ (_____) is the international standard developed by CableLabs that cable operators use to provide Internet access over their existing _____ (_____) infrastructure.

What two types of equipment are required to send digital modem signals upstream and downstream on a cable system?

Match the definition on the left with a term on the right. Terms are only used once.

Definitions

   a. Combining both fiber-optic and coax cabling together into a hybrid cabling infrastructure

   b. Defines the communications and operation support interface that permits the addition of high-speed data transfer to a traditional cable TV system

   c. The direction of a signal transmission from the headend to subscribers

   d. Located in the headend (and communicates with CMs located in subscriber homes)

   e. The rate at which current (voltage) cycles (computed as the number of waves per second)

   f. The direction of a signal transmission from subscribers to the headend

Terms

_____ CMTS

_____ DOCSIS

_____ Downstream

_____ Frequency

_____ HFC

_____ Upstream

DSL

Digital subscriber line (DSL) technology takes advantage of the additional bandwidth available in telephone networks between 3 KHz and 1 MHz.

Briefly describe the two main types of DSL.

The local loop connection to the CO must be less than _____ miles (_____ km).

What two components are required to provide a DSL connection to the teleworker?

The analog voice and ADSL signals must be separated to avoid interference. What two devices can separate the signals?

Match the definition on the left with a term on the right. Terms are only used once.

Definitions   Terms

a. Located at the CO, a device that combines   _____ ADSL
individual DSL connections from subscribers
into one high-capacity link to an ISP   _____ DSL

b. Sometimes referred to as the DSL modem,   _____ DSLAM
a device that connects the subscriber to the
DSL network   _____ Microfilter

c. The category of DSL technology that provides   _____ SDSL
high-speed downstream data capacity value
with a lower upstream capacity value   _____ Transceiver

d. Device with one end connecting to a telephone device and the other end connecting to
the telephony wall jack

e. Category of DSL technology that provides
equal high-speed downstream and upstream
data capacities

f. A means of providing high-speed connections
over pre-existing installed copper wire infrastructure

Broadband Wireless

Of the three broadband technologies, wireless offers the largest variety of ways to connect. Whether from your laptop or from a smartphone, urban or rural, broadband wireless has a solution.

Match the definition on the left with a term on the right. Terms are only used once.

Definitions   Terms

a. Uses a point-to-multipoint topology to pro-   _____ 3G/4G Wireless
vide wireless cellular broadband access at
speeds up to 1 Gbps   _____ LTE

b. Newer and faster technology for high-speed   _____ Municipal WiFi
cellular data (considered to be part of 4G)
_____ VSAT

c. Cellular broadband access that gets faster with   _____ WiMAX
each generation
_____ Wireless Internet

d. Employs a mesh network with an access
points at each node for 802.11 connections

e. A general term for Internet service from a
mobile phone or any other mobile device that
uses the same technology

f. Two-way satellite Internet using IP multicast-
ing technology

Selecting Broadband Solutions

Ideally, a teleworker would have a fiber-optic cable directly connected to the home office. When selecting the broadband solution that is right for you, you want to consider several factors. In Table 15-3, indicate the factors for each broadband solution.

Table 15-3   Broadband Solutions: Factors to Consider

Factor to Consider	Cable	DSL	Fiber-to-the-Home	Cellular/ Mobile	Wi-Fi Mesh	WiMAX	Satellite
Requires fiber installation directly to the home.							
Coverage is often an issue, bandwidth is limited, and data may not be unlimited.							
Bit rate is limited to 2 Mbps per subscriber, cell size is 1 to 2 km (1.25 mi).							
Bandwidth is shared by many users, and upstream data rates are often slow.							
Limited bandwidth that is distance sensitive, and the upstream rate is proportionally quite small compared to downstream rate.							
Expensive, limited capacity per subscriber; often provides access where no other access is possible.							
Most municipalities do not have a mesh network deployed; if it is available and the SOHO is in range, it is a viable option.							

Configuring xDSL Connectivity

The underlying data-link protocol commonly used by Internet service providers (ISPs) to send and receive data across DSL links is PPP over Ethernet (PPPoE).

PPPoE Overview

For the ISP, what are the benefits of using PPP?

What are the three stages of evolution in teleworker connections from the home that use PPP?

Configuring PPPoE

Although PPPoE configuration is beyond the scope of the course, understanding how PPPoE is implemented will help solidify your skills in configuring PPP.

The two steps to configure PPPoE are as follows:

Step 1.   Create a PPP tunnel using dialer interface with the following settings:

- Encapsulation is PPP.

- IP address is negotiated.

- MTU size is set to 1492. Why?

_____

_____

- Dialer interface is assigned a pool.

- CHAP authentication with username and password assigned by ISP.

Step 2.   Enable PPPoE on the interface attached to the DSL modem and assign it as a PPPoE client using the dialer pool defined in Step 1.

You can verify the dialer interface was assigned an IP address with the **show ip interface brief** command.

In Figure 15-1, the ISP router is already configured. Record the commands to configure the Customer router using the following CHAP information:

Figure 15-1   PPPoE Configuration Topology

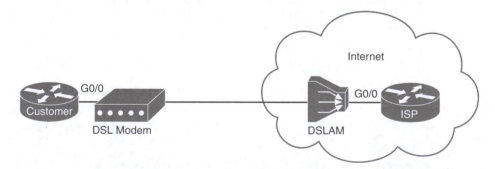

- Username is CustomerBob.
- Password is Bob$connect.

If you want to configure this on lab equipment, connect two routers through a switch or with a crossover cable and use the following configuration for ISP:

```
username CustomerBob password Bob$connect
!
bba-group pppoe global
 virtual-template 1
!
interface GigabitEthernet0/0
 no ip address
 pppoe enable group global
 no shutdown
!
interface Virtual-Template1
 mtu 1492
 ip address 64.100.1.254 255.255.255.0
 peer default ip address pool CUSTOMER_POOL
 ppp authentication chap callin
!
ip local pool CUSTOMER_POOL 64.100.1.1 64.100.1.253
```

Lab - Configuring a Router as a PPPoE Client for DSL Connectivity (CN 6.3.2.3)

CHAPTER 16

Securing Site-to-Site Connectivity

Up to this point in our WAN discussions, we have covered access options, including leased lines, Frame Relay, cable, digital subscriber line (DSL), and wireless. Now it is time to turn our attention toward a popular solution for linking two sites or a teleworker to the corporate office. With the use of generic routing encapsulation (GRE) and IP security (IPsec), virtual private networks (VPNs) play an important role in today's network implementations.

VPNs

With the proper implementation at that central site, VPNs provide the flexibility of having safe and secure connections regardless of the underlying access technology. This is increasingly important as more users need or want access to their corporate networks no matter their current location.

Fundamentals of VPNs

VPNs are used to create a private tunnel over the Internet regardless of the WAN access option used to make the connection.

Briefly describe three different scenarios in which VPNs are a viable solution.

What is the difference between VPN and secure VPN?

To implement a VPN, a VPN gateway is needed. List three devices can serve as a VPN gateway.

Briefly describe four benefits to using VPNs.

Types of VPNs

There are two main types of VPN networks. Site-to-site VPNs support connections where the two locations are permanent and contain more than one user. For example, a branch site or a business partner site most likely would benefit from a site-to-site VPN. Remote-access VPNs are best used for single user connection needs such as teleworkers and mobile users.

In Table 16-1, indicate the type of VPN described by each characteristic.

Table 16-1   Comparing Site-to-Site and Remote-Access VPNs

Characteristic	Site-to-Site VPN	Remote-Access VPNs
VPN is dynamically enabled when needed.		
Most likely uses VPN client software to establish VPN connection and encrypt data.		
Users have no knowledge of the VPN.		

Characteristic	Site-to-Site VPN	Remote-Access VPNs
Connects networks together through peer VPN gateways.		
Uses a client/server model.		
Connects teleworkers and mobile users.		
VPN connection is static.		

Packet Tracer
☐ **Activity**

Packet Tracer - Configuring VPNs (Optional) (CN 7.1.2.4)

Site-to-Site GRE Tunnels

Generic routing encapsulation (GRE) is a site-to-site VPN tunneling protocol developed by Cisco. GRE can encapsulate a wide variety of protocol packet types inside IP tunnels.

Fundamentals of Generic Routing Encapsulation

List three protocols that GRE can encapsulate.

Figure 16-1 shows the basic fields in a GRE encapsulated packet.

Figure 16-1   GRE Encapsulated Packet

Figure 16-2 shows the topology we will use to configure GRE later in this section. Notice how the protocol packet, IP, is encapsulated with GRE, then encapsulated in an IP packet for transport across the Internet. The inside IP packet is using private addressing and the outside IP packet is using public addressing.

Note: The public addressing is on the same subnet. This is uncommon on real networks. However, we are doing it here so that you can easily attach to routers and use this configuration for practice.

Figure 16-2   GRE Topology

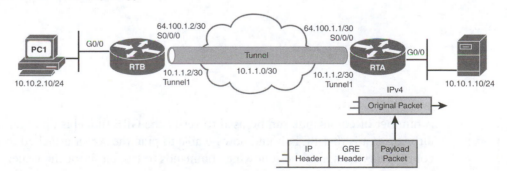

GRE is defined by IETF RFC _____. In the outer IP header, _____ is used in the Protocol field to indicate that a GRE header follows. In the GRE header, a Protocol _____ field specifies the OSI Layer 3 protocol that is encapsulated (IP in Figure 16-2). GRE is _____, meaning that it does not include any flow-control mechanisms. Also, GRE does not include any _____ mechanisms to protect the payload. The GRE header and additional IP header creates at least _____ bytes of additional overhead for tunneled packets.

Configuring GRE Tunnels

In Figure 16-2 shown earlier, assume the physical interfaces on RTA and RTB are configured and active. Also assume that RTA is already configured with a GRE tunnel and OSPF routing. To configure GRE on RTB, complete the following steps:

Step 1.   Create a tunnel interface using the **interface tunnel** *number* command. The interface numbers do not have to match between RTA and RTB.

Step 2.   Configure an IP address for the tunnel interface. The two routers on the tunnel should use addresses from the same subnet. In our topology, the subnet is 10.1.1.0/30.

Step 3.   Specify the tunnel's source IP address in the public part of the network with the **tunnel source** *ip-address* command. The IP address must match the other side's configuration for **tunnel destination** *ip-address*. For RTB, this address is the 64.100.1.2 IP address configured on its S0/0/0 interface.

Step 4.   Specify the tunnel's destination IP address in the public part of the network with the **tunnel destination** *ip-address* command. The IP address must match the other side's **tunnel source** *ip-address*. For RTB, this address is the 64.100.1.1 IP address configured on RTA's S0/0/0.

Step 5.   Configure routing to use the tunnel to advertise the private LANs at each site.

Note: These steps do not include configuring the **tunnel mode** command because the default, GRE IP, is what is needed here. However, in the future, the GRE tunnel will most likely be IPv6.

Using these steps, record the commands including the router prompt to configure RTB with a GRE tunnel to RTA.

A number of commands can be used to verify the GRE tunnel is operational. Of course, the ultimate test is that PC1 should now be able to ping the server attached to the RTA LAN. If connectivity fails, use the following commands to troubleshoot the issue:

Record the commands and command filtering used to generate the following output:

```
RTB# _____


Neighbor ID     Pri   State        Dead Time   Address      Interface
64.100.1.1       0    FULL/  -     00:00:34    10.1.1.1     Tunnel1
RTB# _____
Tunnel1                  10.1.1.2        YES manual up              up
RTB# _____
Gateway of last resort is not set


       10.0.0.0/8 is variably subnetted, 5 subnets, 3 masks
O          10.10.1.0/24 [110/1001] via 10.1.1.1, 00:23:49, Tunnel1
RTB# _____
Tunnel1 is up, line protocol is up
  Hardware is Tunnel
  Internet address is 10.1.1.2/30
  MTU 17916 bytes, BW 100 Kbit/sec, DLY 50000 usec,
     reliability 255/255, txload 1/255, rxload 1/255
  Encapsulation TUNNEL, loopback not set
  Keepalive not set
  Tunnel source 64.100.1.2, destination 64.100.1.1
  Tunnel protocol/transport GRE/IP
    Key disabled, sequencing disabled
    Checksumming of packets disabled
  Tunnel TTL 255, Fast tunneling enabled
  Tunnel transport MTU 1476 bytes
<output omitted>
RTB#
```

In the output from the last command shown, why is the maximum transmission unit (MTU) set at 1476 bytes?

Lab - Configuring a Point-to-Point GRE VPN Tunnel (CN 7.2.2.5)

Packet Tracer - Configuring GRE (CN 7.2.2.3)

Packet Tracer - Troubleshooting GRE (CN 7.2.2.4)

Introducing IPsec

Although GRE is excellent for creating a tunnel across the Internet, it does not include any kind of security. This section reviews basic IPsec concepts. IPsec configuration is not a CCNA Routing and Switching exam topic. So, any practice you do is purely optional.

Internet Protocol Security

RFC 4301, *Security Architecture for the Internet Protocol*, defines IP security, or simply IPsec. Briefly describe each of the four critical functions of IPsec security services.

- Confidentiality (encryption):

- Data integrity:

- Authentication:

- Anti-replay protection:

IPsec Framework

Encryption protects data confidentiality and integrity. Authentication ensures that the sender and receiver actually know and trust each other.

Encryption

What two factors impact the degree of confidentiality in an encryption algorithm?

What is the main difference between symmetric and asymmetric encryption?

In what scenarios are symmetric and asymmetric encryption used?

What is the main purpose of the Diffie-Hellman (DH) algorithm?

Hash-based Message Authentication Code (HMAC) is a mechanism for message authentication using hash functions. A keyed HMAC is a data integrity algorithm that guarantees the integrity of a message.

What are the two common HMAC algorithms?

Briefly describe the operation of an HMAC algorithm.

Authentication

Encryption is crucial, as we have seen. However, a VPN tunnel must also authenticate the device on the other end before the path can be considered secure. Briefly describe the two main peer authentication methods.

-

-

Figure 16-3 is a depiction of the IPsec framework with all the possible algorithm choices for each piece in the framework.

Figure 16-3   IPsec Framework

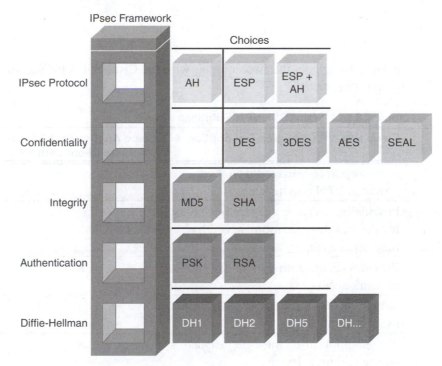

Briefly describe each of the following:

IPsec framework protocol:

Confidentiality:

Integrity:

Authentication:

DH algorithm:

Packet Tracer
☐ Activity

Packet Tracer - Configuring GRE over IPsec (Optional) (CN 7.3.2.8)

Remote Access

As discussed earlier in this chapter, VPNs are an ideal remote-access solution for many reasons. Secure communications can easily be implemented, scaled, and tailored to the access rights of the individual. This section briefly reviews types of remote-access VPN solutions.

Remote-Access VPN Solutions

What are the two primary methods for deploying remote-access VPNs?

List three benefits or features of Cisco SSL VPN solutions.

In Table 16-2, label the two columns with the Cisco SSL VPN solution that is best described by the statements.

Table 16-2   Cisco SSL VPN Solutions

Cisco SSL VPN Solution Description	Cisco AnyConnect Secure Mobility Client with SSL	Cisco Secure Mobility Clientless SSL
Non-corporate-managed devices are provided VPN remote access		X
Provides access to corporate resources for devices that are not managed by the corporation		X
Provides clients with a LAN-like full network access	X	
Remote users establish the SSL session using a web browser		X
A client application must be installed on the end-user device	X	
Requires a standalone application be installed on the end-user device	X	
Access to services is limited to browser-based file-sharing resources		X

IPsec Remote-Access VPNs

The Cisco Easy VPN solution feature offers flexibility, scalability, and ease of use for both site-to-site and remote-access IPsec VPNs. The Cisco Easy VPN solution consists of three components. Label each based on the following descriptions.

- _____: A Cisco IOS router or Cisco ASA firewall acting as a VPN client

- _____: An application supported on a PC used to access a Cisco VPN server

- _____: A Cisco IOS router or Cisco ASA Firewall acting as the VPN head-end device in site-to-site or remote-access VPNs

IPsec exceeds SSL in many ways. In Table 16-3, indicate whether the characteristic belongs to SSL or IPsec.

Table 16-3   Comparing SSL and IPsec

Characteristic	SSL	IPsec
40- to 256-bit key-length encryption.		
Access to all IP-based applications.		
Any device can connect.		
One- or two-way authentication.		
Specifically configured devices can connect.		
Shared secrets or digital certificates for authentication.		
Web applications and file sharing.		
56 to 256-bit, key-length encryption.		

Packet Tracer - Skills Integration Challenge (CN 7.5.1.2)

CHAPTER 17

Monitoring the Network

Most of your CCNA studies have focused on implementing networking technologies. But what if there is currently no design or implementation to do in your job as network administrator? What if the network is already up and running? Then chances are you will be responsible for monitoring the network. Over the years, several tools have evolved to help you do just that. This chapter focuses on three popular monitoring tools: Syslog, Simple Network Management Protocol (SNMP), and NetFlow.

Syslog

The most common method of accessing system messages that networking devices provide is to use a protocol called syslog.

Syslog Operation

Developed in the 1980s and documented as RFC 3164, syslog used UDP port ___ to send notifications across IP networks to a syslog server. Briefly describe the three main syslog functions.

-
-
-

List the four destinations these messages can be sent to.

-
-
-
-

Because you have configured many routers by now, one of the more common messages you have seen is the interface "up" and "up" message, as shown in Example 17-1.

Example 17-1   Syslog Message: Interface Is "Up" and "Up"

```
000039: *Nov 13 15:20:39.999: %LINK-3-UPDOWN: Interface GigabitEthernet0/0, changed
state to up

000040: *Nov 13 15:20:40.999: %LINEPROTO-5-UPDOWN: Line protocol on Interface
GigabitEthernet0/0, changed state to up
```

In Table 17-1, use the second line of output from Example 17-1 to provide an example of each field in the syslog message format.

Table 17-1   Syslog Message Format

Field	Example
Sequence Number	
Timestamp	
Facility	
Severity	
Mnemonic	
Description	

By default, the Sequence Number field is not shown. Record the command, including the router prompt, to add this field to syslog messages.

What are the two different methods to make sure the timestamp is accurate?

Configuring Syslog

Using the topology and addressing shown in Figure 17-1, record the commands including the router prompt to configure the logging service on RTA with the following requirements:

- All logging messages should be sent to the console and to the buffer as well as the syslog server.

- Only log messages with severity 5 or lower.

- The source interface for logged messages should always be the G0/0 interface.

Figure 17-1   Syslog Configuration Topology

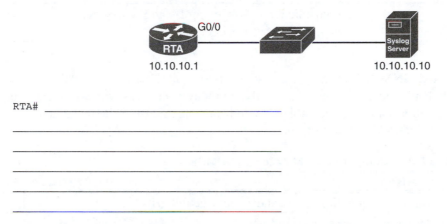

RTA# _____

_____

_____

_____

_____

_____

What command will display the messages logged to RAM?

_____

Lab - Configuring Syslog and NTP (CN 8.1.2.6)

Packet Tracer - Configuring Syslog and NTP (CN 8.1.2.5)

SNMP

SNMP began with a series of three RFCs back in 1988 (1065, 1066, and 1067). The SNMP name is derived from RFC 1067, *A Simple Network Management Protocol*. Since then, SNMP has undergone several revisions.

SNMP Operation

SNMP is an _____ layer protocol that provides a standardized way of communicating information between SNMP agents and SNMP managers using UDP port _____. The SNMP manager is part of a network management system (NMS).

The SNMP manager can collect information from agents using _____ messages. Each agent stores data about the device in the _____ (_____) locally so that it is ready to respond to these messages from the NMS. Agents can also be configured to forward directly to the NMS using _____ messages.

In Table 17-2, indicate the SNMP message type for each of the descriptions provided.

Table 17-2   SNMP Message Type

Operation	Description
	Retrieves a value from a specific variable.
	Retrieves a value from a variable within a table. The SNMP manager does not need to know the exact variable name; a sequential search is performed to find the needed variable from within a table.
	Retrieves large blocks of data, such as multiple rows in a table; only works with SNMPv2 or later.
	Replies to messages sent by an NMS.
	Stores a value in a specific variable.
	An unsolicited message sent by an SNMP agent to an SNMP manager when some event has occurred.

Although SNMPv1 is legacy, Cisco IOS supports all three versions. All versions of SNMP use SNMP managers, agents, and MIBs. In today's networks, you will most likely encounter SNMPv3 or SNMPv2c. In Table 17-3, indicate whether the SNMP characteristic applies to SNMPv2c, SNMPv3, or both.

Table 17-3   Comparing SNMPv2c and SNMPv3

Characteristic	SNMPv2c	SNMPv3	Both
Used for interoperability and includes message integrity			
Provides services for security models			
Uses community-based forms of security			
Includes expanded error codes with types			
Provides services for both security models and security levels			
Authenticates the source of management messages			
Cannot provide encrypted management messages			
Supported by Cisco IOS software			X

In SNMPv1 and SNMPv2c, access to the MIB is controlled through the use of two types of _____:

■

■

Why is this type of access no longer considered best practice?

The MIB defines a variable using a MIB object ID. These IDs are derived hierarchically using the scheme shown in Figure 17-2. Label Figure 17-2 with the most common public variables.

Figure 17-2   Management Information Base Object ID Scheme

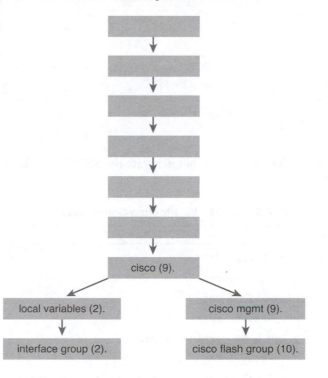

cisco (9).

local variables (2).

interface group (2).

cisco mgmt (9).

cisco flash group (10).

 Lab - Researching Network Monitoring Software (CN 8.2.1.8)

Configuring SNMP

In Figure 17-3, RTA is an SNMP agent and NMS is an SNMP manager. Record the commands to configure SNMPv2 on RTA with the following requirements:

- Use an ACL to allow NMS read-only access to the router using community string **NMS_eyesonly.**

- Location is **Aloha_Net** and the contact is **Bob Metcalfe.**

- Specify that 10.10.10.10 is the recipient of traps and explicitly configure the router to send traps.

Figure 17-3   SNMP Configuration Topology

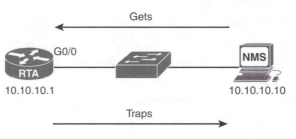

Gets

G0/0

NMS

RTA

10.10.10.1

10.10.10.10

Traps

```
RTA(config)#
```

Record the commands that generate the SNMP verification output for RTA shown in Example 17-2.

Example 17-2   SNMP Verification Commands

```
RTA# _____

Chassis: FTX163283RZ

Contact: Bob Metcalfe

Location: Aloha_Net

0 SNMP packets input

    0 Bad SNMP version errors

    0 Unknown community name

    0 Illegal operation for community name supplied

    0 Encoding errors

    0 Number of requested variables

    0 Number of altered variables

    0 Get-request PDUs

    0 Get-next PDUs

    0 Set-request PDUs

    0 Input queue packet drops (Maximum queue size 1000)

0 SNMP packets output

    0 Too big errors (Maximum packet size 1500)

    0 No such name errors

    0 Bad values errors

    0 General errors

    0 Response PDUs

    0 Trap PDUs

SNMP Dispatcher:

   queue 0/75 (current/max), 0 dropped

SNMP Engine:

   queue 0/1000 (current/max), 0 dropped


SNMP logging: enabled

    Logging to 10.10.10.10.162, 0/10, 0 sent, 0 dropped.
```

```
RTA# _____


Community name: ILMI

Community Index: cisco0

Community SecurityName: ILMI

storage-type: read-only        active



Community name: NMS_eyesonly

Community Index: cisco1

Community SecurityName: NMS_eyesonly

storage-type: nonvolatile      active access-list: SNMP



Community name: NMS_eyesonly@1

Community Index: cisco2

Community SecurityName: NMS_eyesonly@1

storage-type: nonvolatile      active access-list: SNMP
```

NetFlow

Although syslog and SNMP are powerful tools for collecting information about networking devices, owners of networks were looking for a tool to measure TCP/IP flows. So, Cisco engineers developed NetFlow, which quickly gained popularity in the marketplace.

NetFlow Operation

What is the latest version of NetFlow called?

What improvements does it make over the original version?

Briefly describe four reasons to use NetFlow.

- ■

- ■

- ■

- ■

NetFlow is not a replacement for SNMP. Both have their purposes in network monitoring. In Table 17-4, indicate whether the characteristic describes SNMP or NetFlow.

Table 17-4   Comparing SNMP and NetFlow

Characteristics	SNMP	NetFlow
Agents can send traps to a network management system when defined events occur.		
Access to the MIB is controlled through community string settings.		
An external server (collector) is used to record IP network monitored cache changes.		
Interface errors, CPU usage, and memory usage are not recorded.		
A Management Information Base (MIB) is used to record network monitored events.		
Collects IP data to record who used network resources and for what purpose those resources were used.		

Define a TCP/IP flow.

What fields in a packet are used to determine that the packet is from a different flow?

Configuring NetFlow

To implement NetFlow on a router, complete the following steps:

Step 1.   Configure NetFlow to capture inbound and outbound packets.

Step 2.   Configure where to send NetFlow data.

Step 3.   Verify NetFlow is operational.

Using Figure 17-4 as a reference, record the commands configure RTA to capture and send NetFlow data from interface G0/0 to the collector using Version 9.

Figure 17-4   NetFlow Configuration Topology

```
RTA(config)#
```

Record the commands that generated the NetFlow verification output on RTA shown in Example 17-3.

Example 17-3   NetFlow Verification

```
RTA# _____
GigabitEthernet0/0
  ip flow ingress
  ip flow egress
RTA# _____
IP packet size distribution (132959 total packets):
   1-32   64   96  128  160  192  224  256  288  320  352  384  416  448  480
   .998 .000 .000 .000 .000 .000 .000 .000 .000 .000 .000 .000 .000 .000 .000


    512  544  576 1024 1536 2048 2560 3072 3584 4096 4608
   .000 .000 .000 .000 .000 .000 .000 .000 .000 .000 .000


IP Flow Switching Cache, 278544 bytes
  1 active, 4095 inactive, 32 added
  728 ager polls, 0 flow alloc failures
  Active flows timeout in 30 minutes
  Inactive flows timeout in 15 seconds
IP Sub Flow Cache, 34056 bytes
  1 active, 1023 inactive, 28 added, 28 added to flow
  0 alloc failures, 0 force free
  1 chunk, 1 chunk added
  last clearing of statistics never
Protocol         Total    Flows   Packets Bytes   Packets Active(Sec) Idle(Sec)
--------         Flows    /Sec    /Flow   /Pkt    /Sec    /Flow       /Flow
UDP-other           13    0.0     10225    32     37.4    17.6        15.5
ICMP                18    0.0         1   181      0.0     0.1        15.0
Total:              31    0.0      4288    32     37.4     7.5        15.2
```

```
SrcIf          SrcIPaddress    DstIf          DstIPaddress     Pr SrcP DstP  Pkts

SrcIf          SrcIPaddress    DstIf          DstIPaddress     Pr SrcP DstP  Pkts
Gi0/0          10.10.10.10     Local          10.10.10.1       01 0000 0303    1
RTA# _____
Flow export v9 is enabled for main cache
  Export source and destination details :
  VRF ID : Default
    Destination(1)  10.10.10.10 (2055)
  Version 9 flow records
  63 flows exported in 29 udp datagrams
  0 flows failed due to lack of export packet
  0 export packets were sent up to process level
  0 export packets were dropped due to no fib
  0 export packets were dropped due to adjacency issues
  0 export packets were dropped due to fragmentation failures
  0 export packets were dropped due to encapsulation fixup failures
```

 Lab - Collecting and Analyzing NetFlow Data (CN 8.3.3.3)

CHAPTER 18

Troubleshooting the Network

In an ideal world, networks would never fail. But mechanical failures happen. Users of the network do unexpected things. So, issues will arise that require a network administrator's effective troubleshooting skills—one of the most sought after skills in IT. This chapter reviews network documentation, general troubleshooting methods, and tools.

Troubleshooting with a Systematic Approach

Documentation is the starting point and is a crucial factor in the success of any troubleshooting effort. With documentation in hand, a network administrator can choose a troubleshooting method, isolate the problem, and implement a solution.

Network Documentation

List three types of documentation a network administrator should have to effectively troubleshoot issues.

List at least four pieces of information that could be included in a network device's configuration documentation.

List at least four pieces of information that could be included in an end system's configuration documentation.

In Table 18-1, indicate whether the feature is part of a physical topology document or logical topology document.

Table 18-1   Physical and Logical Topology Features

Feature	Physical Topology	Logical Topology
WAN technologies used		
Interface identifiers		
Connector type		
Device identifiers or names		
Cable specification		
Operating system version		
Cabling endpoints		
Device type		
Data-link protocols		
DLCI for virtual circuits		
Site-to-site VPNs		
Static routes		
Cable type and identifier		
Routing protocols		
Connection type		
IP address and prefix lengths		
Model and manufacturer		

As you learned in Chapter 17, "Monitoring the Network," the purpose of network monitoring is to watch network performance in comparison to a predetermined baseline.

What is the minimum duration for capturing data to establish a baseline?

When is the best time to establish a baseline of network performance?

In Table 18-2, indicate which statements describe benefits of establishing a network baseline.

Table 18-2   Benefits of Establishing a Network Baseline

Statements	Benefit	Not a Benefit
Enable fast transport services between campuses		
Investigate if the network can meet the identified policies and use requirements		
Combine two hierarchical design layers		
Locate areas of the network that are most heavily used		
Identify the parts of the network that are least used		
Identify where the most errors occur		
Establish the traffic patterns and loads for a normal or average day		

When documenting the network, it is often necessary to gather information directly from routers and switches using a variety of **show** commands. Match the information gathered on the left with the show command on the right.

Information Gathered

a. Contents of the address resolution table

b. Uptime and information about device software and hardware

c. Detailed settings and status for device interfaces

d. Summary of the NetFlow accounting statistics

e. Contents of the routing table

f. Summarized table of the up/down status of all device interfaces

g. Summary of VLANs and access ports on a switch

h. Current configuration of the device

Command

_____ **show ip route**

_____ **show arp**

_____ **show vlan**

_____ **show ip interface brief**

_____ **show running-config**

_____ **show version**

_____ **show interface**

_____ **show ip cache flow**

Packet Tracer - Troubleshooting Challenge - Documenting the Network (CN 9.1.1.8)

Troubleshooting Process and Methodologies

All troubleshooting methodologies have four stages they share in common: three stages to find and solve the problem and a final important stage after the problem is resolved. In Figure 18-1, label the four major stages in the troubleshooting process.

Figure 18-1   Major Troubleshooting Stages

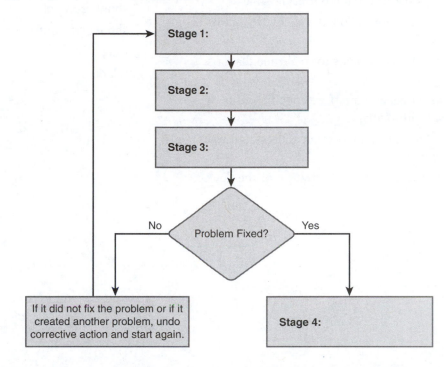

Note: The Academy curriculum does not label the last stage as Stage 4. However, that is most likely an oversight. Stage 4 is indeed the final and arguably most important stage.

The gathering symptoms stage can be broken into five steps:

Step 1.   Gather information

Step 2.   Determine ownership

Step 3.   Narrow the scope

Step 4.   Gather symptoms from suspect devices

Step 5.   Document symptoms

In Step 1, you will most likely use a variety of commands to progress through the process of gathering symptoms. In the following activity, match the information gathered with the testing command.

Information Gathered

    a. Displays a summary status of all the IP Version 6 interfaces on a device

    b. Shows the path a packet takes through the networks

    c. Displays the IP version 6 routing table

    d. Connects remotely to a device by IP address or URL

    e. Offers a list of options for real-time diagnostics

    f. Shows global and interface specific status of Layer 3 protocols

    g. Sends an echo request to an address and waits for a reply

    h. Shows the current configuration of the device

Testing Command

_____ show running-config

_____ debug ?

_____ traceroute

_____ show ipv6 interface brief

_____ show protocols

_____ show ipv6 route

_____ ping

_____ telnet

In Table 18-3, identify the troubleshooting methodology described by each statement.

Table 18-3   Troubleshooting Methodologies

Statements	Bottom Up	Top Down	Divide Conquer	Shoot from the Hip	Spot the Difference	Move the Problem
Disadvantage is it requires you to check every device and interface						
Begins at the OSI application layer						
Use an experienced troubleshooting guess to investigate a possible cause						
Used for problems that likely involve software settings						
Compare a working and nonworking situation while looking for the significant differences						
Use when suspected problem is cabling or device failure						
Begins at the OSI physical layer						
Swap the problematic device with a known-working device						
Start with an informed guess for which OSI layer to begin troubleshooting						
Disadvantage is it requires you to check every network application						

Network Troubleshooting

Effective troubleshooting requires good tools and systematic approaches. The section reviews some of the tools used in today's networks and some specific troubleshooting symptoms at various OSI layers.

Troubleshooting Tools

A wide variety of software and hardware tools is available to make troubleshooting easier. You can use these tools to gather and analyze symptoms of network problems. Match the description on the left with the tool on the right.

Description

a. Online repositories of experience-based information

b. Discovers VLAN configuration, average and peak bandwidth utilization using a portable device

c. Tools that document tasks, draw network diagrams, and establish network performance statistics

d. Measures electrical values of voltage, current, and resistance

e. Tests data communication cabling for broken wires, crossed wiring, and shorted connections

f. Powerful troubleshooting and tracing tool that provides traffic tracking as it flows through a router

g. Provides a graphical representation of traffic from local and remote switches and routers

h. Analyzes network traffic, specifically source and destination frames

i. Includes device-level monitoring, configuration, and fault management

j. Tests and certifies copper and fiber cables for different services and standards via a handheld device

Software and Hardware Tools

_____ Host-based protocol analyzer

_____ Cable tester

_____ Portable network analyzer

_____ Baseline establishment tool

_____ Cable analyzer

_____ Network Management System Tool

_____ Cisco IOS Embedded Packet Capture

_____ Knowledge Base

_____ Network Analysis Module

_____ Digital multimeter

Network Troubleshooting and IP Connectivity

A network administrator should be able to quickly isolate the OSI layer where an issue is most likely located. In Table 18-4, indicate the most likely layer associated with each issue.

Table 18-4   Isolating the OSI Layer Where an Issue Resides

Network Problems and Issues	OSI Layers				
	1	2	3	4	5, 6, and 7
A computer is configured with the wrong default gateway.					
The DNS server is not configured with the correct A records.					
Traffic is congested on a low capacity link and frames are lost.					
STP loops and route flapping are generating a broadcast storm.					
A cable was damaged during a recent equipment install.					
ACLs are misconfigured and blocking all web traffic.					
SSH error messages display unknown/untrusted certificates.					
The **show processes cpu** command displays usage way beyond the baseline.					
A VPN connection is not working correctly across a NAT boundary.					
A static route is sending packets to the wrong router.					
The routing table is missing routes and has unknown networks listed.					
On a PPP link, one side is using the default Cisco encapsulation.					
SNMP messages are unable to traverse NAT.					

Knowing which command to use to gather the necessary information for troubleshooting is crucial to effectively and efficiently resolving problems. All the commands you have mastered over the course of your CCNA studies are part of your troubleshooting toolkit. This next exercise only highlights a few.

Match the command output on the left with the command on the right.

Command Output

    a. Displays all known destinations on a Windows PC

    b. Displays all known IPv6 destinations on a router

    c. Can be used to verify the transport layer

    d. Clears the MAC to IP address table on a PC

    e. Displays the MAC to IP address table for other IPv6 devices

    f. Displays the known MAC addresses on a switch

    g. Displays input and output queue drops

    h. Displays the IP addressing information on a Windows PC

Command

_____ show ipv6 neighbors

_____ ipconfig

_____ show ipv6 route

_____ telnet

_____ show mac address-table

_____ arp -d

_____ route print

_____ show interfaces

Note: No book or study guide will effectively teach you how to troubleshoot networks. To get proficient at it, you must practice troubleshooting on lab equipment and simulators. This practice works best with a partner or a team because (1) you can collaborate together to resolve issues and (2) you can swap roles, taking turns breaking the network while the other person or team resolves the issue. For those readers with access to the Academy curriculum, the Packet Tracer activities in this chapter are great resources for just such practice sessions with your team. But you also know enough now that you can create your own troubleshooting scenarios to try out on each other. There is no doubt that you will be asked to trouble-shoot several issues on the CCNA exam. So, practice as much as you can now in preparation for the test. You might be surprised how fun and rewarding it can be.

Packet Tracer
☐ Activity

Packet Tracer - Troubleshooting Enterprise Networks 1 (CN 9.2.3.12)

Packet Tracer - Troubleshooting Enterprise Networks 2 (CN 9.2.3.13)

Packet Tracer - Troubleshooting Enterprise Networks 3 (CN 9.2.3.14)

Packet Tracer - Troubleshooting Challenge - Using Documentation to Solve Issues (CN 9.2.3.15)

Packet Tracer - CCNA Skills Integration Challenge (CN 9.3.1.2)

CISCO
Cisco Learning Network
Free Test Prep and Beyond.
Access review questions
Watch Quick Learning Modules (QLMS)
Search for jobs and network with others
Take self-assessments
Participate in study groups
Play online learning games
Register for a free membership
and get started now.
www.cisco.com/go/learningnetwork
Cisco Learning Network
A social learning site brought to you by Learning@Cisco